MUSIC AND FR

By the same Author

Elgar: A Life in Photographs 1972
Elgar on Record: The Composer and the Gramophone 1974
A Voice in Time: the Gramophone of Fred Gaisberg 1976

Photo: Crispian Woodgate

Music and Friends

Seven decades of letters to
ADRIAN BOULT
from
Elgar, Vaughan Williams, Holst,
Bruno Walter, Yehudi Menuhin
and other friends

Annotated by Jerrold Northrop Moore

FOREWORD BY KEITH FALKNER

'It has always been my chief object to perform everything as if it
were the finest piece of music I have ever known. It follows
from this that I can have no favourites.'

HAMISH HAMILTON
LONDON

First published in Great Britain 1979
by Hamish Hamilton Ltd
Garden House, 57–59 Long Acre, London WC2E 9JZ

British Library Cataloguing in Publication Data

Music and friends.
  1. Music – Miscellanea
  I. Moore, Jerrold Northrop   II. Boult,
Sir Adrian
  780   ML90

  ISBN 0–241–10178–6

Phototypeset by Western Printing Services Ltd, Bristol
Printed and Bound in Great Britain by
Redwood Burn Ltd, Trowbridge and Esher

CONTENTS

ILLUSTRATIONS

Half-tone plates between
pages 128 *and* 129

'The conductor speaks': an early BBC television programme from the Alexandra Palace, 14th May 1939.

Conducting the Vienna Symphony Orchestra, 26th March 1947.

Recording the Vaughan Williams Symphonies, Kingsway Hall, December 1953: Adrian Boult with Ursula and Ralph Vaughan Williams.

Listening to tapes at the EMI Studios, 1978. In the past fourteen years Sir Adrian has made over sixty recordings with Christopher Bishop, producer (*left*), and Christopher Parker, balance engineer.

'To dearest Adrian with devoted love from his no-longer-so-young colleague Yehudi, November 7, 1962.'

In the text

FOREWORD

These letters from 1911 to 1978 paint a fascinating picture of Music in this century. They range from Adrian Boult's lecture at the age of twenty to Jonathan Del Mar's discussion with him of a Karajan (Beethoven) performance in 1978. Perhaps most interesting of all are the letters from Gustav Holst and Ralph Vaughan Williams giving such insight into their work.

From beginning to end one is conscious of the great affection and belief in Sir Adrian Boult and his integrity as an artist. First with the elderly, later with professional and amateur musicians and now with the rising generation.

This is not the place for personal reminiscence and gratitude which I, and so many decades of musicians, would wish to record. Yet, I must tell of the Centennial Concert for 'H.P.A.' we gave in 1969 at the R.C.M. Sir Adrian conducted the final piece – 'Dona nobis pacem' from the B minor Mass. It was as though his eye and the point of his stick had hypnotised us and was certainly one of the finest moments in music-making I have known. When Frank Howes, hardened critic though he was, wrote of the emotional impact the performance made on him I realised once again it had been no ordinary happening.

Alas! we shall not be under his 'benign baton' again in public but it is good to know he has many recording sessions to come. When Sir Adrian telephones his friends and begins with 'I say!' we know the call is of a personal and social nature. But when he says, 'I say, look here!' we know that matters of great moment are afoot.

In 1909 he put conductors into three classes; those who beat time – Richter; those who guide – Safonoff; and those who hypnotise – Nikisch. Sir Adrian favours Safonoff but the Nikisch magic is surely there too. 'Of all the British conductors I have heard, Boult is the one who moves me most; *even in Brahms*.' So said Josef Krips to me in Vienna a few years ago.

Sir Adrian. A great conductor and a great man. His way of life is summed up in the final words of *Music and Friends*.

KEITH FALKNER

ACKNOWLEDGEMENTS

One day in March 1978 Sir Adrian rang to ask if I would like to see a group of letters which had just turned up, written to him by Elgar fifty and sixty years ago. The Elgar correspondence emerged as a small part of a rich accumulation of letters to Adrian Boult from every sort of musician from almost the beginning of the century. There were several extensive correspondences with composers and other conductors. Altogether it amounted to a virtual history of orchestral music in this country since the First World War. The letters had not been used for Sir Adrian's autobiography *My own trumpet* published by Hamish Hamilton six years ago. The conclusion was obvious, and I made it: to arrange a companion volume from a chronological selection of these letters. This is the book, published on 9th April 1979 – Sir Adrian's 90th birthday.

Sir Adrian and Lady Boult smiled ruefully on the project. But they have given generously of the help which only their memories and diaries could supply. The rest of the history's value has come from the friends pictured within. Imogen Holst has been unstinting in her help over her own letters, those of her father, and those of the late Vally Lasker, and has in several cases provided Sir Adrian's replies. Ursula Vaughan Williams has done the same for her letters and those of her husband. Yehudi Menuhin opened a wonderful file of letters he has received from Sir Adrian over the years. A rich documentation of the B.B.C. years was made available by Mrs Jacqueline Kavanagh and her staff at the B.B.C. Written Archives Centre – where history is understood so well that the historian finds himself truly helped.

Grateful thanks are due also to:
Sir Richard Allen, for permission to reproduce letters from Sir Hugh Allen, Sir Robert Armstrong, Sir Thomas Armstrong, the trustees of the estate of Sir Arnold Bax, Mr Christopher Bishop, Lady Bliss for permission to reproduce letters from Sir Arthur Bliss and herself, Mlle Nadia Boulanger, Mme Marta Casals Istomin for permission to

reproduce letters from Senor Pablo Casals, the trustees of the estate of Sir Walford Davies, Mr Jonathan Del Mar, the Delius Trust, the trustees of the Sir Edward Elgar Will Trust, Mr W. H. Fellowes for permission to reproduce letters from E. H. Fellowes, Dr Howard Ferguson, Mr Carl Flesch, Dame Margot Fonteyn de Arias, Mr Emil Gilels, Sir Bernard Haitink, Mr Ernest Hall, Mr Edward Heath, the Paul Hindemith Institute, Frankfurt-am-Main, the family of the late Frank Howes, Mrs Norah Kirby for permission to reproduce letters from Dr John Ireland, Mr Michael Kennedy, Lord Maclean, Sir Robert Mayer, Lord Ponsonby of Shulbrede for permission to reproduce letters from Sir Hubert Parry, Mr Robert Ponsonby, Mr Christopher J. Reith for permission to reproduce letters from Sir John (later Lord) Reith, E.M.I. Ltd for permission to reproduce a letter from Sir Landon Ronald, the executors of the estate of Mr Harold Samuel, Mr Rudolf Schwartz, the Society of Authors on behalf of the G. B. Shaw estate, Dr Harold Watkins Shaw, Mr Bernard Shore, the estate of Dame Ethel Smyth, Solomon, M. Paul Tortelier, the trustees of the estate of Sir Donald Tovey, Mr Barry Tuckwell, Sir Michael Tippett, Sir William Walton, Mr Malcolm Williamson and Lady Jessie Wood for permission to reproduce letters from Sir Henry J. Wood and herself.

The postcard from George Bernard Shaw reproduced on page 99 is copyright © 1979 The Trustees of the British Museum, the Governors and Guardians of the National Gallery of Ireland and the Royal Academy of Dramatic Art.

Every effort has been made to trace the owners of copyright in letters quoted in this book; any omission is regretted.

Jerrold Northrop Moore

Hampstead, 7th October 1978.

MUSIC AND FRIENDS

PROLOGUE

In his second year at Oxford, in November 1909, Adrian Boult addressed the Oriana Society in a talk modestly called 'Some notes on performance'. It is an astonishing achievement for a 20-year-old, surveying the whole question of performance, its whys and where-fores, its past and its future. He welcomes the gramophone (which he finds attaining 'a very fair state of perfection'), but deplores its small use as a documentor of serious music. He treasures interpreta-tion by composers themselves, while mistrusting the 'traditions' of their followers. And then comes his justification of the new men:

> The men who are alive at the inception of a great work of art can only assimilate a small portion of its greatness, leaving what they cannot see or understand for generations of their successors to evolve; performances becoming more and more perfect as the work gets older. Now a performance of this kind is a new reading in the highest sense of the term.

He lays down three precepts for an ideal performance – observance of the composer's every wish, clarity through an emphasis on bal-ance and structure, a final effect of music made utterly without effort. They have been the precepts of his career through the ensuing seventy years. The paper concludes with a magisterial survey of the London orchestras and conductors to be heard in 1909 – a survey which history has confirmed in every detail.

When the President honoured me with an invitation to read a paper to this Society, I tried to think of a subject (on which I felt capable of speaking) which would embody those *general principles* which several older members have noticed usually lead to the most interesting discussions. Perhaps a few points

1

on performance, which have occurred to me from time to time, may be found to serve this purpose.

Performance is of course by far the more important of the two ways in which the musical thoughts of one being are assimilated by others. The reading of written music, though it brings about a far more thorough grasp of the work under consideration, is of necessity only possible for the comparatively few people who have trained themselves to *hear* what they really only see; and it is through *performance* that music 'comes to its own' and makes its appeal to music lovers in general.

And yet, although performance is essentially the *public* side of the art – for as often as not the composer is not recognised till after his death, and even while alive he is not usually present at performances of his works – the name of the performer does not live long, his work is ephemeral, and he is only remembered so long as those who have heard him survive to tell of his readings. So it is that there can be no traditions in performance. Everything changes – the quality and often the whole system of the instrument, the surroundings and acoustic properties of the music-room, and above all the intelligence and point of view of the performer himself, until the performance of music much more than one hundred years after its inception under so-called 'original conditions' seldom has an interest more than historical, and even then the interpretation is controlled by modern and not contemporary brains.

An invention which will actually show our great grandchildren exactly how we perform our things today has recently been brought to a very fair state of perfection. It is a pity that this – the gramophone – is being confined almost entirely to extracts from operas or drivelling ballads, sung by so-called star singers at a time when the art of singing is perhaps in a worse condition than it has been since the science of voice-production was first considered.

There is another aspect of tradition to which it will not be out of place to give some thought, and it will be best shown

2

by an example. The Vienna Philharmonic Orchestra was recently described as consisting of men whose fathers had played under Brahms, grandfathers under Beethoven, and great grandfathers under Mozart and Haydn, and so performed the music of these masters in the exact manner desired by them – holding the traditions first hand. That the tradition here meant is only that small part of it which is worth holding is obvious to anyone who has heard the orchestra. As we saw before, their instruments and theatres are different, all they keep is the spirit of the composer and his work, and even this is continually altered by the increasing intelligence of the successive generations, and also by the thought and temperament of the many conductors who have since directed the orchestra, and of whom at any rate all the best will have left their mark on the playing of the men.

Another example of the same sort would be the Munich Wagner Festival, where all that is good in Wagner's system remains and is made more and more effective by the different people who play their part in it, whereas at Bayreuth the masterful hand of Frau Wagner holds the tradition so tight that the best artists will not appear there now, so hampered are they by her foolish insistence on the letter rather than the spirit of her husband's art.

With regard to the old masters this question of tradition in performance is another aspect of the test of time. Two composers live in the same town at the same time. Opinion is divided as to their respective merits. To all but the most discerning of their contemporaries they are equal; but there is in the work of the one nothing underneath for subsequent generations to discover, whereas the other, quietly working with the assurance of a genius, is giving to the world masterpieces which will survive for centuries. The oldest music is only beginning to be appreciated by the most modern study of it – Dr. Allen is continually showing us new beauties in Bach and Palestrina, beauties of which the composers may have been conscious or only subconscious, but which must have been lost on their contemporaries, and it is only after the most careful consideration and the deepest appreciation of all

3

these that – given adequate technique – these old masters can nowadays make any general appeal. The men who are alive at the inception of a great work of art can only assimilate a small portion of its greatness, leaving what they cannot see or understand for generations of their successors to evolve; performances becoming more and more perfect as the work gets older.

Now a performance of this kind is a new reading in the highest sense of the term. Nothing can be more abominable than the hysterical straining after false effect, the exaggeration of unimportant detail, and the consequent loss of the main points and object of the work, which one hears only too often in London under the guise of a new reading, and it is lamentable that the very men who have done much in their young days for the advancement of the art, and the revival of works which have seemed long dead, should, like Hans von Bülow, become so eccentric later on in their careers as to commit the very crimes they would have fought against when younger.

I should now like to submit for examination and probably correction, what I consider to be some of the principles of a good new reading, and I think that a test of their soundness will be their application to performances of modern works, thus making them what we may venture to call (standard) rules.

1. They must give the hearer the impression that they are being played exactly as the composer wished.

To my first hearing of Bach's 3rd Brandenburg Concerto (in G for 10 part strings) under Fritz Steinbach of Meiningen fame, I had come steeped in the Bach Gesellschaft edition, which, as you know, has practically no expression marks; and I was amazed to find expression in every bar. There were crescendos, and diminuendos which I suppose would have been put in naturally and perhaps only subconsciously by every member of the orchestra had he been a born Bach player, but which, failing this, had been most carefully prepared by the conductor. This edition is now published in the miniature score, and although of course it would be far better

4

if all this feeling came naturally from every performer, it is impossible to expect this from any ordinary orchestra, and so the use of the Steinbach edition seems to me an almost perfect way of performing the work provided that the marks are not made the object of the whole performance, but only the means of exhibiting and explaining its beauty as a work of art.

Now take the modern test. It is my firm belief from experience – though of course this extends a very short way – that composers are the best performers of their own work. The generally-accepted theory that composers never can play or conduct their own things is, in my opinion, entirely due to the fact that a great many of them do not take the trouble to make themselves technically efficient, or else that they cannot exercise the self-control necessary when appearing before an audience. Tschaikovsky's nerves were always too much for him, and I believe our own Elgar has, as a conductor, had accidents for the same reason, but whenever I have heard him, he has always struck me as singularly impressive and convincing. Of other composers, though Grieg suffered from extreme nervousness, Fauré, Weingartner, Paderewski and Max Reger have all done most ample justice to their own works, and I have heard Strauss, Debussy, Weingartner and Sibelius conduct fairly familiar things of their own better than anyone else. Saint-Saëns was less successful from lack of technique as a conductor, but his piano and organ playing of his own compositions is, from all accounts, quite perfect. Our English composers Parry, Stanford and Mackenzie cannot be expected to do themselves justice if their experience includes (as I believe to be the case) nothing but isolated performances of their own works.

2. The second principle is that the reading must be *clear*. Ruskin's rule that in drawing there should be no line which bears no meaning, is applicable equally to music. In the perfect work there is not a note without its point, without its part to play in the general scheme. In the perfect performance each of these is brought out in its true relation to every other, and not one is obscured. The Steinbach performance I spoke of before, besides making one feel that Bach himself could

not have done it better, made one understand each point in his work, and see the reason for each step that he took. The balance of solo and *tutti*, the balance of keys, the structure of each movement and the whole concerto were all laid out before us and again each part rose and fell as if it had been a separate instrument of totally different timbre, with the advantage of the unity produced by the similarity of tone of all the strings. This is a quality which Dr. Allen has given his choirs. Each horizontal part rises and falls in its own place without losing the vertical or harmonic effect. A performance of this class makes the analytical programme unnecessary. It tells you more than volumes of analysis.

Clearness is an essential of modern quite as much as of classical polyphony. The apparent isolation of each part is a very noticeable feature of the readings of such different conductors as Richter, Nikisch, Safonoff, and the playing of men like Ysaÿe, Pugno, Bühlig is just as remarkable for the way in which the whole work seems held together by the balance of its keys and movements, and is, as it were, opened out, so that each point in the work, and the relation to every other, can be taken in at a single glance.

3. Another principle is that the work must *sound easy*. In solo work, of course, this depends chiefly on technique. However much a man may know or think about the music he is playing, he cannot make it sound easy unless his fingers will do exactly what his brain requires. (The wonderful piano playing of Mr. Nikisch, who seems to get through the most enormously difficult accompaniments as if they were child's play, seems like an exception to this, but here we have a man who knows exactly his own adequate, though comparatively small, technical power, and who will not hesitate to alter the letter of the work to suit his fingers, without in the least disturbing the spirit, or general effect.) However, as the number of parts in the work increases, technique becomes less indispensable, a thorough understanding of the work serving to show each performer how to play his own part, and the most difficult ensemble will sound easy and the most elaborate polyphony simple.

With modern music it is just the same. A man I know once said that had his first hearing of a Brahms Symphony been a performance by the Meiningen Orchestra under Steinbach, he would have confidently recommended it to any amateurs as well within their capabilities!

Having essayed to lay down the law with regard to performance in general, I had now intended to take the separate branches of the art from solo music to opera, and try to show some points to be borne in mind in the performance of each in particular. On starting, however, I found it was an enormous undertaking, especially for one whose experiences are as limited as my own, and I shall therefore confine myself to the three in which I have hitherto been chiefly interested, namely: song, duets for two pianos, and the orchestra.

Song

To begin with song. In my opinion there are very few singers indeed who give enough attention to the poetic side of their work. The primary inception and the whole working out of the idea is the poet's. He dictates the style of treatment, the structure, and even the sequence of keys to the composer, who is merely adorning and perhaps amplifying the work, giving, as it were, a commentary on it in another language. So surely the first consideration for the singer is to make every syllable easily audible to every member of the audience. How many singers are there now before the public, who come very near perfection in every other respect, temperament, beauty and adaptability of tone, who even make their singing highly expressive to anyone who has the words before him, but what is this to the man who does not happen to have paid sixpence for his book of words, and what, at private concerts, where there are usually no books of words? So long as our good and even mediocre poets refuse to have anything to do with translation, leaving it – in almost every case – to the cheapest of cheap versifiers to bring the finest thoughts of foreign poets and musicians within reach of the great majority of Englishmen, true artists must sing the songs in their original lan-

7

guages, and must give their audiences the words and translations thereof, but this is no excuse for neglecting to make the words clearly audible to anyone who can understand the original language. Let us have good translations of songs, and let our singers learn how to enunciate them properly.

But this question no way lessens the importance of the accompanist. Indeed, clear declamation from the singer will give the pianist more chances of bringing forward the beauty of his share of the work which, in the more modern type of song, is a very large one, and it is the greatest pity for the accompanist to reduce himself to a nonentity, even when playing the simplest accompaniments. Even an Alberti bass can and should be made interesting.

The relations of singer and accompanist will necessarily alter the more they work together. It is always as well, when first playing for a singer, to obscure the accompaniment, as any unexpected action on his part can be much more easily met. But as time goes on the pianist can emerge until he attains a perfection of balance like that of Mme. Kirkby Lunn and Mr. Percy Pitt, or Mr. and Mrs. Hamilton Harty, or of Miss Gerhardt and Mr. Nikisch. This last, of course, is a rather exceptional case as Mr. Nikisch, I believe, coaches Miss Gerhardt very carefully beforehand and can then, at the performance take his place as nothing more than a sympathetic accompanist.

When I hear singer and accompanist working so well together I always wonder why a little more interest is not given by the pianist to the modulation which usually connects songs in the same group. We read how Mendelssohn, playing two *Songs without Words* at the Gewandhaus, took the accompaniment figure of the first and gradually changed it into that of the second, modulating all the time into the new key;* and I

*This is exactly what Wagner does in the majority of cases to connect two scenes of the same Act. The curtain falls on music full of the motive of the previous scene, then gradually new themes appear until the curtain rises again to music illustrative of the next scene.

remember someone telling me how M. Paderewski mystified a Liverpool audience by similarly connecting up a group of Chopin. I cannot say exactly how he did it; it is not hard to mystify a Liverpool audience.

Another point of great interest in connection with song is: may a singer transpose a song, or should he avoid all those whose original compass does not correspond to his own?

A short while ago I should have emphatically answered this with 'original key or not at all' – but I was recently much upset by a discussion I had on this point, and I am inclined to think now that in certain cases transposition does not affect the expression of the song, provided the new key is judiciously chosen, although I must confess that there is much which is intolerable in any key but that of its inception.

Two Pianos

A very much neglected, and undeservedly neglected, form of chamber music is the duet for two pianos. Its possibilities and many delightful qualities have been explored by almost all the great composers from Bach to Max Reger, and the fact that they all wrote for the combination in a totally different way points to the enormous variety and extent of its range. Brahms' arrangements of his symphonies are in themselves such magnificent works of art that no one could object to hearing them as such, and the versions of the F minor Quintet and Haydn Variations (the latter was actually finished in this form before it was orchestrated) are amongst the finest things in the whole realm of music. With the F minor particularly – on hearing it as a quintet it seems impossible that an arrangement of it for two pianos could ever sound anything but an arrangement, and yet, so perfectly has it been done that the duet seems a new work, and quite unsuitable for a quintet. Nevertheless the two versions are extraordinarily close. Amongst quite modern works, Saint-Saëns' Scherzo – in which he makes much use of the tonal scale, so dear to modern France, and Max Reger's wonderful Variations on a theme of Beethoven which was so enthusiastically praised by

9

Paderewski, are well worth consideration, while Sir Hubert Parry has given us more than one contribution to this form of art.

An interesting question with regard to two-piano music is that concerning the pianos – should they be what might be called twins, that is of the same make and age, or should they differ? I have never played on any but pianos of very different tone, and one certainly feels more interest sometimes when echoing a tune from the other piano, in making it as like as possible, leaving the timbre of the instrument to give the variety.

This is a sensation quite peculiar to two-piano music. In the works of the older masters, and also the fascinating *Romance and Variations* by Grieg, a tune is often repeated by one piano immediately after the statement by the other – but to make this effective the first must always remember that the second is coming, and must continue, without making his passage sound dull, to leave room for enough extra interest to be added by the second piano to avoid the feeling of anti-climax produced by a weaker repetition or of dullness produced by one exactly similar.

The performances of two ladies who visited London some years ago can hardly be classed with two-piano music. They restricted their programmes almost entirely to arrangements of solo works which they played on twin pianos in such a manner as to make it difficult to believe that more than one piano was being used, and impossible to distinguish the parts – a wonderful tour de force but artistically no better than if they had played the original solo piece in unison.

The Orchestra

Concerning the orchestra there is a great deal to discuss as it is, in its present condition, the youngest of the forms of musical expression, and has not up to the present found itself any basis on which to continue its development on the new lines. By this I do not mean to imply that in itself it has altered, except in the quality of the instruments and intelligence of the performers; also, of course, in the many and varied instruments added to their scores by the modern extremists, but it is from our present point of view that the orchestra is entering upon a fresh stage of development. The advent of the virtuoso conductor has changed it from a more or less confused collection of different units into a single and completely controllable body of men – the finest instrument in the world, because it is alive. It is this question of control, and how it is to be exercised that is, I think, the most interesting of all we are considering tonight, but first I should like to look at the orchestra itself.

In London three years ago there were, for all practical purposes two orchestras. The one, a musical republic, ruled itself, and was directed by anyone and everyone; for their own concerts the committee chose distinguished foreigners, and when playing for others their conductor was chosen for them. The other, consisting entirely of the servants of a limited company, always played under Mr. Wood, except on the rare occasions when foreign composers came to conduct their own works. The London Symphony, although only about four years old, had been led by almost every conductor of note, and had already taken its place among the very finest orchestras, its extraordinary flexibility and quickness in meeting the wishes of its new conductors being universally recognised and commended. The Queen's Hall band, however, was and is a permanency, and will always remain firmly fixed in the readings of Mr. Wood or whoever may succeed him. Since the time we are speaking of two more orchestras have been formed, both on the lines of Mr. Wood's, and the greatest provincial orchestra – Dr. Richter's – is also the same. But surely this is wrong – it cannot be good for the orchestra, for where is the conductor who can ever do justice to all the different schools of orchestral music? – and it certainly is not good for the conductor to have no change of interest and environment. In Germany, I understand, the permanent conductors are continually visiting other orchestras, thereby relieving the monotony for both. Again the expense of moving orchestra and instruments makes it extremely difficult for

11

other towns ever to get a chance of hearing men like Mr. Wood, Mr. Beecham and Mr. Ronald, if they refuse to leave their orchestras. The financial failure of the visits of the Hallé Orchestra to London, and the difficulty a lesser light than Dr. Richter has recently found in conducting his (Richter's) band are significant examples of both these points, which, I think, are distinctly pointing to the fact that the orchestra of the future is a flexible instrument, permanently situated in each town – and let us hope to see one soon in every town in England – visited continually by different conductors, British and foreign.

If this is to be the future of the orchestra, into what is the conductor developing? The conductors of the present day may be divided into three schools: there are the men who beat time, like Dr. Richter; who guide the orchestra, like M. Safonoff; and who hypnotise the orchestra, like Mr. Nikisch. It seems treason to say anything against Dr. Richter, but I must confess that I cannot help feeling that he is the last of his line. No one who has ever heard him can forget the magnificent breadth, dignity and power of his performances of the classics, and his steady beat which produces an absolutely even tempo, unbroken sometimes from beginning to end of the longest symphonic movement. But this is all he does at performance. All the expression he wishes for – usually exactly what is indicated and nothing more – is arranged at rehearsal, and this, of course, implies that the orchestra is used to his ideas, or that he has had more rehearsals than are usually practicable at the present day. The London Symphony have from the beginning shown themselves wonderfully quick to grasp his meaning, but they are an exceptional orchestra, and even they would probably find difficulty in playing well under a man of Richter's school who had anything less than Richter's personality. This type of technique, then, is past, except, perhaps, when controlling an amateur orchestra, whose life is almost as much in rehearsal as in performance.

The second school to consider is that which, for want of a better word, I have described as guiding the orchestra. Here

12

the impression is that the conductor is leaving the orchestra to supply their own force and interpretation, himself only giving occasional suggestions for them to follow, and it is just in these suggestions that he brings the orchestra to his own way of thinking and his personality and impression of the work is stamped on the players, and thence on the audience, with far more life and power than if the reading had been cut and dried at rehearsal.

At the head of this school of conductors stands, I think undeniably, M. Wassili Safonoff. His power lies in the freedom he gives the orchestra, and it is this very freedom which enables them to obey him absolutely – paradoxical though it may seem. At the most impressive moments I have seen him fold his arms and watch the work go on, as Mendelssohn used, with perfect effect. The question of his using or not using a bâton does not bear much on his control of the orchestra, but it seems to me that the stick will almost invariably lead the conductor into beating time, a pure waste of energy with the modern orchestra, and therefore that the use of the hand is better as a far more suitable medium of expression.

The third school is exceptional, and I only know one man who can be said to belong entirely to it. But hypnotism or personal magnetism plays such an important part in conducting that anyone who makes use of it to such an enormous extent as Mr. Nikisch does, must be studied very carefully. It is, of course, incompatible with the performance of anything but music of the most nervous and intensely emotional character – *Tristan* being perhaps his best work – but in things of this kind his grip of the orchestra is so complete that he is able to alter the tempo several times in one bar without the slightest loss of ensemble. So long is his bâton (over two feet) that by a turn of the wrist he can keep the players at boiling point without sacrificing that complete repose which is so essential to complete control.

Nikisch, as I have said, is the only conductor who uses practically nothing but magnetism to gain his effects, and even if others like him were to appear, they could never give adequate performances of the classics (Nikisch's Haydn, it

13

must be remarked, is quite perfect in its way, but Mr. Hadow has shown us how far removed Haydn is from the classical spirit). Again, Dr. Richter's style is almost impossible to apply to music of the emotional order; so we are left with the school of Safonoff, as that on which the art of conducting is to develop. As far as I know this is borne out by the practice of most of the great conductors of today. Richard Strauss is one, although in emotional music – particularly his own – he tends rather in the direction of hypnotism. Weingartner is another who seems to let the orchestra have their own way – at the same time he has a wonderful control over them. Most of the others too are of this school, although many are hampered by feeling the necessity of beating time as well – by this I mean a careful insistence on every beat of the bar – whereas a slight indication of the first beat is surely all that is necessary with the modern orchestra.

The virtuoso conductor, then, is developing into the man who will guide the orchestra. He must be endowed with a large measure of magnetism, and if he feels that by this he can lead the orchestra to emotional crises in the style of Nikisch where such are suitable, by all means let him do it, provided he does not have to exaggerate his gestures. If this should be necessary and he is physically exhausted at the end of a work, let him moderate his energy; for over-emphasis must bring about enormous loss of power.

I trust I have not bored the Society by this lengthy and rambling statement of my views of performance. They have been formed always from the audience and not the platform of the concert-room, and must necessarily be one-sided, and also, I expect, in many cases wrong. At any rate I hope that there are some here who will from experience on the other side of the footlights give us better and more mature views on some of the exceedingly interesting questions on which I have been bold enough to express an opinion.

I. A Youth for British Music
(1911–1929)

Letters began to be written to Adrian Boult in the 1890's. At his family's home in Blundellsands, Lancashire, and later at The Abbey Manor, West Kirby, notes and letters came from parents occasionally absent, from his sister, from friends. More letters arrived through school days at Westminster – where in 1901 he became a regular subscriber to Henry Wood's Sunday Concerts at the Queen's Hall and began the habit of attending with the scores to note down points of interpretation. At Christ Church, Oxford, in the autumn of 1908 he astonished the Dean by stating his intention to become an orchestral conductor, and then set about persuading Professor Hugh Allen to let him sing in the Oxford Bach Choir's B minor Mass virtually without rehearsal.

In all these places Adrian Boult's presence invited letters of affection and intimacy. But the life of a conductor is the most public of musical lives. So the letters in this book are from the people with whom he worked and made his career. One of the first was Samuel Augustus Barnett, whose philanthropic vision created the Hampstead Garden Suburb:

About two years before I came to the end of my time at school, Canon Samuel Barnett was transferred from Bristol to Westminster by Sir Henry Campbell-Bannerman's government. Barnett and his wife, later Dame Henrietta, were already leaders of many Liberal movements . . . Old friends of my parents, they were very kind to me and I met many eminent people at [No. 3, The Little] Cloisters . . . I saw the early plans [for the Hampstead Garden Suburb] on the floor of their drawing-room . . .[1]

At the end of 1911 there was the chance of a few weeks' tutoring. Canon Barnett stood referee.

[1] Sir Adrian Boult, *My own trumpet* (Hamish Hamilton, 1973), pp. 82–3.

3, The Little Cloisters, Westminster Abbey.
Dec.12.11

Dear Adrian.

Will this character do? It is what I shld want in a man for my boys. I cld have said how kind you are to old folks & a great deal more but I expect this is enough. I hope you are going to get through all right

Ever yrs
Saml A Barnett

Mr Adrian Boult has been known to me fr. his childhood upwards. His character is such as to qualify him for a tutorship in wh. his high sense of honour & his good nature wld surely influence his pupils for good.

Saml A Barnett
Canon of Westminster Abbey

After taking his Mus.Bac. at Oxford in 1912, Adrian Boult fulfilled an old dream of spending a year at Leipzig – where Nikisch directed the Gewandhaus Orchestra, though he had retired from teaching the conducting class at the Conservatory. Boult nonetheless put himself down for the Conservatory classes in Theory and composition, Singing, Piano playing and Score playing and conducting (under Nikisch's successor Hans Sitt). This he described a few years later for a journalist, who wrote:

The method of training conductors at that famous Conservatoire he found was as follows. You entered the score-reading class, and started by playing a Bach Chorale from score at your lesson. You got through without more than a brief comment. Next time you got on rather better perhaps, but whether better or worse was nobody's particular concern except your own. You went on playing Chorales. By degrees you were advanced to a string quartet, still later to a quintet, a sextet, and so on. And *after two years* (of teaching yourself) you were admitted to the weekly conducting class.

Here you found yourself one of twelve or fourteen students who had to be 'got in' during the two hours. When your name was called, you sprang up to confront a (very bad) orchestra consisting of half the strings and all the wind in the Conser-

16

vatoire. Once in the conductor's desk, you were like a swimmer in a stormy sea battling his way to shore. No rope of advice was ever flung, no pause allowed. Dare to call a halt, and a stentorian bellow from the end of the hall hounded you on. And when you emerged panting and dazed from the breakers, no discussion of your difficulties or mistakes ever ensued to help you.

The Fresher who had bearded Dr. Allen, however, was not likely to be overawed by the conventions of the Leipzig Conservatoire, and whereas the good young German would have meekly followed the prescribed course, the good young Englishman somehow 'wangled' things so that he got Hans Sitt to let him into the Conducting Class after six weeks! Having justified his admission by managing at his first wielding of the baton to correct three false entries without stopping the band, no objection could be made to his remaining in his unlawful position, so study proceeded apace.[1]

In July 1913 Adrian Boult obtained his certificate:

Theory of Music & Composition (Principal Subject) Mr Boult, who is very industrious and gifted, has acquired remarkable skill both in contrapuntal style and in composition. Songs, pianoforte pieces, etc., testify in the best possible manner to his feeling for melody and sense of form.

Stephan Krehl.

Piano playing. Assisted by good musical knowledge, Mr Boult has worked successfully at laying a foundation and improving his piano technique by the study of finger exercises and études.

Heynsen.

Score playing & Conducting. Mr Boult has attended my lessons regularly and has shown very great gifts especially as a conductor.

Hans Sitt.

Singing. Mr Boult has followed his singing lessons with zeal and attention, has studied the Groundwork of Voice Production (Scheidemantel) with much intelligence, so that he

[1] Katherine E. Eggar, 'The career of Mr. Adrian Boult', in *The Music Student*, January 1921, p. 220.

17

is well prepared to become an instructor. Mr Boult has rendered especial service as a technically reliable accompanist of fine musical feeling.

Eugen Lindner.

He would have liked to go on to Vienna, but an overstrained heart necessitated returning home. During the autumn of 1913 he divided his time between Oxford, where he began reading for the Mus.Doc., and his parents' home at West Kirby. The Boults offered hospitality to many distinguished musicians visiting Liverpool. One of them was the German conductor Max Fiedler. Fiedler was a protégé of Brahms. His brother Hermann had a distinguished academic career in England as Dean at the new University of Birmingham before moving on to the Oxford Professorship of German.

During his visit to the Boults, Max Fiedler was especially interested to hear of the 24-year-old Adrian's plan to conduct his first concert with a professional orchestra. A group of players from the Liverpool Philharmonic had been engaged for a full-length programme at West Kirby on 27th February 1914. In the programme was Hugo Wolf's *Italian Serenade* – placed there deliberately because of the special demands it makes on the conductor. After his visit, but before the West Kirby concert, Max Fiedler wrote from Berlin.

Schillerkolonnade 119, Portal IV, Charlottenburg
Jan. 18 1914

My dear young friend and colleague,

What a thoroughly kind-hearted soul you are! Don't you think, that I did not notice all your tricks and ways of pouring kindness into me! I *did* & I shall always remember it.

If I could only give you some pleasure or help you in some way! Well – could I perhaps in the way of scores?

I know by experience, that one has moments of doubt about tempo, beat etc.; will you promise to drop me a line if such doubts should happen to trouble your mind? I should be so glad to tell you what I know. – I am much interested to hear about your concert – the Italian Serenade is a difficult piece!

With kindest regards to your sister (who carried [secretly] my 'Frack'[1] to the station!!) and to yourself

Yours truly
Max Fiedler.

[1] Dress coat.

Friday, February 27th, 1914.

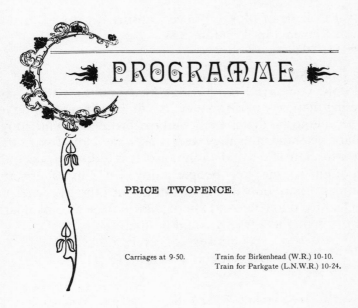

PROGRAMME

PRICE TWOPENCE.

Carriages at 9-50.   Train for Birkenhead (W.R.) 10-10.
Train for Parkgate (L.N.W.R.) 10-24.

Adrian Boult's first concert conducting a professional orchestra. His programme was the Bach Brandenburg Concerto no. 2, 'Martern aller Arten' from Mozart's *Entführung aus dem Serail* (sung by Agnes Nicholls), *The Banks of Green Willow* by George Butterworth, the 2nd and 3rd movements of the Schumann Piano Concerto (with W. B. Brierley as soloist), Wagner's *Siegfried Idyll*, 'Ah! fors' è lui' from Verdi's *La traviata* (sung by Agnes Nicholls), the *Italian Serenade* of Hugo Wolf, and the Overture to Mozart's *Don Giovanni*.

Before the West Kirby concert came the OUDS production of Aristophanes' *The Acharnians*, with music by Sir Hubert Parry. Parry was another occasional guest of the Boults at The Abbey Manor. He had resigned the Oxford Professorship of Music in 1908 to make way for Hugh Allen and pursue his own duties as Director of the Royal College of Music in London. Now Parry returned to Oxford to conduct several performances of *The Acharnians*. Other performances were conducted by Allen, and on 23rd February Adrian Boult appeared in the pit. Parry wrote a letter of congratulation.

Royal College of Music, Prince Consort Road,
South Kensington, London, S.W.
Feb 23, 1914

My dear Boult
  I hope you have been having a real good time today conducting that jolly performance. It's hideously tantalising not to be able to be there. I enjoyed the proceedings mightily – What a splendid crew they were, and what a lot of spirit they put into their jokes and evolutions! It is a thing never to be forgotten. I hope your people enjoyed it. I'm comfortably confident that you will put lots of go into the Music, & am much obliged to you! And I hope there will be no end of larks tomorrow night. I wish I could be there!
                    Yours very sincerely
                    C. Hubert H. Parry

  By the time Boult passed his Mus.Doc. examinations in December 1914, the Great War had begun. Declared unfit for active service by the Medical Tribunal, he put on his uniform of the Oxford Cavalry OTC and began to drill Lancashire miners. This 'amateur soldiering' (as he called it) did not at first interrupt conducting. His special concern, as a young man in a position to present his own concerts, was the difficulty of orchestral musicians thrown out of work by the war:

Before we were moved to St Asaph I was able to organize a few more concerts in Liverpool with an orchestra of about thirty drawn from the Philharmonic, who were very glad of

20

opportunities to play, as people had largely stopped taking lessons.[1]

... I was able to give a series of so-called popular concerts with an orchestra of twenty-nine: eight wood-wind, two horns, two trumpets, one percussion and sixteen strings, and we did anything up to middle Beethoven, and of course modern works for small orchestra. We had no trombones, as I felt more strings would be needed to balance them. The chief problem was to find a bright finish to each programme, as in most works of this kind trombones are indispensable. I used to fall back on Haydn Rondos and Mozart Finales, and it was surprising how happy the audience got over these things. They seemed to enjoy them as much as if they had had a far lighter conclusion to the concert. At any rate the audience which began with 200 (in a Hall which held 4,000!) finished 1,000 strong at the end of ten concerts.[2]

An old family friend, Frederick Marquis, was among the audience for these concerts in the Sun Hall. He was in charge of the University Settlement, a club run by Liverpool University for dockers, and he invited Boult to conduct six further concerts at the University Settlement Theatre in the autumn. But before that Boult found himself proposed for membership in the Society of Composers. His sponsors were Parry and the distinguished tenor Gervase Elwes.

Royal College of Music,
Jany. 21. 1915

My dear Boult
I am pleased and proud to sign your nomination form. I have sent it on to Gervase Elwes.

Your Orchestral Concerts are very enterprising. I hope they will attract good audiences. It is so important to keep Music going in these distracting times – There are lots of people working with that object, and things seem to be gradually setting into normal conditions. Your big scheme will be a

[1] *My own trumpet*, p. 33.
[2] 'The orchestral problem of the future', in *Proceedings of the Musical Association*, Session XLIX (1923), p. 51.

21

notable help. I should like to report it to the Professional Classes War relief Council, which has absorbed the 'Music in Wartime' Committee which is engaged on similar lines. They may possibly have been in communication with you, as they are trying to get reports from all Musical Societies and Concert Givers with the view of gauging the amount of outof-workness there is among musicians, and helping where they can.

I hope your people are all well – Please give them my heartiest greetings.

yours very sincerely
C. Hubert H. Parry

Billing Hall, Northampton.
Jan. 21 1915

My dear Boult,
(Please drop the 'Mr'!)
Thanks for your letter. I have been away the last week which accounts for the tardiness of my answer! I have sent on the paper duly signed by Parry and myself to the Secretary of the Composers' Society.

I think you are doing splendidly in your work – with both recruits and musicians – Four of my boys are serving, at least three are fighting at present, two in the trenches and the third as a Midshipman on the 'Duncan', and the fourth is going out to drive an ambulance in about a week. It is an anxious time! I have recently got back from New York where I was singing in *Gerontius* last month. Please remember me very kindly to your people – Ever yours sincerely

Gervase Elwes

It is indeed good of your Father to wish me to shoot with him next season. I should love it if it were possible.

I was surprised and delighted that the [Liverpool] concerts resulted in an invitation from the very conservative Committee of the Philharmonic Society to conduct a concert for them in January 1916.[1]

[1] *My own trumpet*, p. 33

He asked for some further lessons from Landon Ronald.

The Guildhall School of Music,
John Carpenter Street,
Victoria Embankment, E.C.
October 15th 1915

Dear Mr. Boult,

I have only just received your letter of the 12th inst. on my return to town, which will explain to you my delay in replying to it.

I would be very pleased if I could help you, but you are quite right in surmising that I do not approve of or give lessons in Conducting.

The only thing that I can suggest to you which might be of some slight service is, if in going over the various Scores that you conduct, you come across some technical points about which you are in doubt, you might bring them up to me and pass half an hour or three-quarters and I might be able to make things clear to you that appear difficult.

I have done this with other young Conductors and have been able to help them considerably, but I could not undertake to do it regularly week by week but only on odd occasions.

I am compelled, under the conditions, to ask fees that may be almost considered prohibitive, but my time is so fully occupied and as it is only in very exceptional cases that I do this, I am compelled to charge two guineas for 20 minutes, or in other words, at the rate of £6.6.0 per hour.

Your programmes interested me very much, and if once you came to do anything serious with me, I should have to make an effort to run up and see you conduct somewhere, as then I might be of real service to you by unkind criticism and pointing out your weakness, if you have any.

Give me good notice if you make up your mind to come up and see me during November, and if you do so, pray mark all the points which you want explained in your Scores.

With kind regards, and wishing you every possible success,
Believe me, dear Mr. Boult,
Yours sincerely,
Landon Ronald

23

A six-guinea hour with Ronald produced a good hint: to stop the orchestra, strike the baton on the flat of the desk and not the edge – it will avoid breaking the stick.

Meanwhile war work went on.

When the Reserve Centre office broke up in 1916, I was offered a job in the War Office, concerned with the German Press. Hardly had I begun, when I ran into Fred Marquis, who insisted on my transferring to the War Office branch in Tothill Street where he was gradually assuming control of the country's leather resources. Work as his personal assistant took me almost to the end of the war, and also, with Marquis' permission, enabled me to organize four concerts with the London Symphony Orchestra . . .[1]

The concerts took place at Queen's Hall in February and March 1918. In addition to the classics, their programmes were designed to include the music of British composers young and old. The note was struck at the beginning of the programme notes written especially for the concerts by Edward J. Dent.

There has probably been no age in the history of the civilised world when conservative musicians did not lament, and the younger musicians rejoice, at the thought that they were living in a period when the whole art of music was undergoing a radical change of outlook and method. Certainly we are tempted to take such a view at the present day . . . The new orientation is not confined to any one country, but it has aroused peculiar interest in England, because it happens to have coincided with a sudden outburst of artistic activity not only in music, but in other fields as well. The intellectual and spiritual devastation of the last three years has been the more tragic because in 1914 there could be no doubt that the younger generation of poets, musicians and workers in other arts had at last secured freedom of action and an opportunity for individual development such as their elders had never had the good fortune to know . . .

The first of these 'new' Englishmen in the concerts was Gustav

[1] *My own trumpet*, pp. 34–5.

24

Borough of Shrewsbury.

WAR TIME BOOTS.

Arrangements have been made for a range of samples of War Time Boots to be placed upon the Market by Manufacturers under the general supervision of the War Office.

The Samples will be exhibited in the **General Market Arcade, Shrewsbury,** as follows :—

FRIDAY, 18th January, 1918
SATURDAY, 19th   „   „
MONDAY, 21st   „   „   10-30 a.m. till
TUESDAY, 22nd   „   „   12 noon and 3
WEDNESDAY 23rd   „   „   till 5 p.m.
FRIDAY, 25th,   „   „

MR. A. C. BOULT, an Officer of the Department, will be present between the hours of 2-30 and 4 p.m. on Friday, 18th January, when retailers (in Shrewsbury and the surrounding Districts) are particularly requested to attend with the view of discussing any difficulties, and the representatives of the local press are invited to meet Mr. Boult at 2-30 p.m. on Friday, 18th January.

J. WILLIAMS,
GUILDHALL, SHREWSBURY,   Deputy Town Clerk.
   10th January, 1918.

Brown & Brinnand, Ltd., Printers, Shrewsbury.

Holst – or von Holst as he was still at the beginning of 1918. He was already a friend, as Boult recalled:

At Morley College in the later years of the War he used to give staggering choral and orchestral programmes with the help of a remarkable type of voice called 'war tenor'. . . . In particular I [remember] a mock opera in five acts, culminating in Debussy and Wagner . . .[1]

The first of the LSO concerts, on 4th February 1918, included Holst's *Country Song* (from *Two Songs Without Words*).

S[t.] P[aul's] G[irl's] S[chool]
Feb 5 [1918]

Dear Boult

Everybody is wild with enthusiasm over your beautiful rendering of the Country Song. Please accept my (a) thanks (b) blessing (c) congratulations. I hope you were satisfied. It's a splendidly plucky enterprise of yours and I do hope you'll get adequate support.

I hope to come to the rehearsal on the 16th and on March 3d.

We are singing Madrigals at Morley on March 2nd at 7.30. Will you come and bring 1) your voice 2) Weelkes vols X XI XII XIII 3) any tenor who can read 4) any other singer who can ditto 5) any body who wants to listen?

On Feb 23d at 7 we are performing a new work 'English Opera as she is wrote' in six acts and five languages (one of them being tonic solfa).

If you'd like to write a notice of it for the [Morley College] Mag we'd be grateful.

If you'd like to act in the chorus (Italian brigands disguised as food inspectors) you must come to rehearsal on the 22d.

The best of luck to your enterprise
                    Yr
                    GVH

[1] 'Gustav Holst: the man and his work', in *The Radio Times*, 15th June 1934, p. 819.

The next concert, on 18th February, included an early performance of *A London Symphony* by Ralph Vaughan Williams. The programme would begin with Elgar's Overture *In the South*. Adrian Boult had first talked to Elgar at the home of their friend Frank Schuster when he was at Westminster, and had attended many important Elgar performances through the intervening years. Now he went up to Elgar's home in Hampstead on the day before the rehearsal and concert. Lady Elgar wrote in her diary:

February 17 . . . Mr. Boult to tea. Quite a nice quiet man. E. went through *In the South* with him – He seemed really to understand. Raid in evening – lasted rather a long time.
February 18. E. & A. to Queen's Hall at 10.30 – to hear Mr. Boult rehearse *In the South*. Too few strings but reading of it really good. Feared audience wd. be almost none on account of raids, & so it was . . .

'At the end of the concert', the young conductor remembered, 'orchestra and audience (about equal numbers) collected in the basement bar at Queen's Hall until the "All clear" had sounded.'[1] But Elgar inscribed the score from which Boult had conducted *In the South*, and Vaughan Williams wrote enthusiastically about the performance of the *London Symphony*.

R.A. Mess, St. Lucia Barracks, Bordon, Hants.
Feb 25 [1918]

Dear Boult
    In all the hurry of Monday I never had an opportunity of thanking you (1) for doing my symph
                (2) for giving such a fine performance – it really was splendid you had got the score right into you & through you into your orch:
    May I say how much I admired your conducting – it is real *conducting* – you get just what you want & *know* what you want & your players trust you because they know it also – I heard many expressions of admiration from both audience and performers (von Holst & A. Hobday among others) – of course you are an experienced conductor by now & your

---

[1] 'England for music', in *The Star*, 4th April 1935.

27

power is well known to many – but to me who have been out of music for 3 years it was new – Good luck to you – I look for great things in the future when such musical ability & such public spirit go hand in hand

                  Ys er
                  R Vaughan Williams

They were already going hand in hand. The small audience determined Adrian Boult to make room in the last of his four programmes on 18th March for another performance of the *London Symphony* – for which he suggested some cuts. Vaughan Williams was particularly concerned that nothing should displace the work of his friend George Butterworth, *A Shropshire Lad*, also down for performance in the Boult concerts. Butterworth, killed on the Somme in 1916, was the dedicatee of the *London Symphony*.

Leith Hill Place, nr. Dorking
Sunday [3rd March 1918]

Dear Boult

Thank you very much for your letter – I shd be proud for any part of the L.S. to be done again by you – but you certainly mustn't cut about your programme for it – especially not the *Shropshire Lad* which ought to be heard everywhere as often as possible.

I agree with you that the last movement & possibly the scherzo of my Symph are too long – but it is *re-writing* they want – I do not think that mechanical cutting – however skilfully done wd. be satisfactory – Why not do the 1st. movement only? It stands fairly well by itself.

I fear I shall be far away on March 18th as I am down for overseas & may leave any day now

                  Ys vy sincerely
                  R. Vaughan Williams.

The third London Symphony programme included Parry's *Symphonic Variations*. Boult asked whether Parry would come to the rehearsal.

28

Royal College of Music, Prince Consort Road,
South Kensington, London, S.W.7
Febry.27.1918.

My dear Boult

Thank you very much! It's very kind of you. I'll come with
pleasure on Sunday morning. I've had such sad experiences
with those variations that I think it's being on the safe side to
say that I hope you spotted that the tune is very slow. One
man who did them a little while ago started at a jaunty
Allegro, and so amazed me that I have never got my breath
back when I think of it!!! I could only suppose there was
something wrong in the way I had written it. It ought to feel as
if it were 8 in a bar, $\downarrow$ = about 62. Forgive my safeguarding the
situation.

Yours very sincerely
C. Hubert H. Parry.

And with all the safeguarding, Boult recalled,

. . . When I referred to him at the rehearsal he asked for it 'still
slower', and as he vigorously sang the tune he made even the
semiquavers sound strong and independent.[1]

The performance on 4th March 1918 drew a last fond tribute from
the old man.

Royal College of Music, Prince Consort Road,
South Kensington, London, S.W.7
March 5 1918

My dear Boult

I am much beholden to you for a surprisingly good performance of those ancient Variations. They all bucked up splendidly and put their backs into it, and deserve my hearty
thanks. I congratulate you on the good hold you have on the
performers and the insight & spirit of your interpretations –
and I hope you enjoy it thoroughly.

It was a great pleasure to see your sister again. I have been

[1] *My own trumpet*, p. 20.

disappointed at not being able to keep in touch with your people. They were so kind & so congenial.

Yours very sincerely
C. Hubert H. Parry

The 4th March programme also included Butterworth's *A Shropshire Lad* and the first concert performance of extracts from the ballet *Between Twelve and Three* by Arnold Bax.

10 Heath Hurst Rd. Hampstead. N.W.3.
Wednesday [6th March 1918]

My dear Boult

I am writing to thank you for your performance of the ballet the other night. It went excellently, except for the fact that the side drum was apparently seized with a maenad fury, so much so that he was unable to contain himself and poured out his dithyrambic soul in places where his entry was merely on the horizon. I always did think that Schroeder[1] was Bacchic.

I meant to see you afterwards, but had to rush for a train. By the way what has happened to the Score and parts? have they been sent to 7 Cavendish Sq?

Yours Arnold Bax

The centrepiece of the final concert, on 18th March, was the repeat performance of the Vaughan Williams *London Symphony*. As a whole, the series made a deep impression in spite of small audiences. Before it began, Adrian Boult's name had been so little known in London that the LSO Board required a reference from the Liverpool Philharmonic Society before agreeing to the concerts. After the final programme *The Musical Times* summarised:

Thus closed a bold venture which was not nearly supported by the public as it should have been, but which has served to establish the reputation of Mr Boult in London as an orchestral conductor of high rank. If every musician of influence in the country could do so much for native art as Mr Boult has done during this season, the outlook would be happier than it is.

[1] J. Schroeder, percussionist of the London Symphony Orchestra.

Soon he was in correspondence with Sir Henry Wood over the *London Symphony*:

c/o Captain Willink Burneside Kendal
July 29:1918.

Dear Mr. Boult

I am so sorry never to have replied to your very kind letter about the Full Score of the Vaughan Williams Symphony, but I have got very much behind hand in my correspondence, but I am hoping to cope with some of it, during my two weeks holiday up here.

I only want the V.W. score for a few days, in order to see how much rehearsal it will require in London & the provinces & I can only judge this by looking it through.

Unfortunately I missed both your splendid performances of it. Could you arrange for me to have a look at it, anytime after my return to town on August 10th, or shall I communicate with Mrs. Vaughan Williams & save you all further trouble & bother (perhaps you can oblige me with her address on a postcard) – but it is a precious score & must not be trusted to the post.

May I be allowed to offer you sincerest congratulations upon your recent splendid series of Orchestral Concerts; the programmes were most interesting, & I hear on all sides, that you made a great personal success

Believe me
Sincerely yours
Henry J. Wood

P.S. Do let me have the cuts.
[P.]P.S. How very kind of you to write me about the Boston appointment, it was hard to refuse, but I felt it was a patriotic duty to remain in my own country, at the present moment, & in my long interview with Mr. Balfour only a few weeks ago, he quite sympathised with me in my ideas.

Wood had been invited to become conductor of the Boston Symphony Orchesta, but with the war still on, his place he felt was at home.

One day in mid-September there was a sudden visit from Gustav Holst. The subject was his unperformed masterpiece *The Planets*.

'I've been ordered to Salonika in a fortnight, and Balfour Gardiner has given me a wonderful parting present. It consists of Queen's Hall, full of the Queen's Hall Orchestra, for the whole morning on Sunday week. We're going to do *The Planets* and you're going to conduct.'

So spoke a wide-eyed visitor to a certain war-worker a few weeks before the Armistice. The news thus broken, work had to begin in real earnest. The parts had to be copied – most of St. Paul's Girls' School seemed to be doing that, as the score was luckily in separate volumes; the conductor coached, chiefly by means of [the] arrangement for two pianofortes, which was played on several evenings by Miss Vally Lasker and Miss Nora Day after a day of war work or part copying; the chorus trained – this was fairly easy, as they all came from St. Paul's or Morley College and knew all about it in good time for the performance.

I remember the night before the performance some of us were dining together and discussing the score when Geoffrey Toye pointed to figure III in 'Neptune' (where the brass are playing *pp* chords of E minor and G# minor together) and said:

'I'm sorry, Gustav, but I can't help thinking that's going to sound frightful.'

'Yes, I know,' was the reply; 'it made me shudder when I wrote it down, but what are you to do when they come like that?'[1]

It was a combined rehearsal and informal performance on that Sunday morning, 29th September 1918, from 10.30 to 1.30 p.m. The stalls were reserved for the choir, the circle nearly filled by the invited audience. The result was a triumph for everyone concerned. Afterwards Adrian Boult was approached by Norman O'Neill, Hon. Treasurer of the Philharmonic Society, with an invitation to direct two of their concerts during the coming season. Sir Henry Wood, who had heard Boult conduct for the first time, was deeply

[1] 'Gustav Holst: the man and his work', in *The Radio Times*, 15th June 1934, p. 819.

impressed, as he himself was to write: 'To direct such a score, which was very complicated, was a great achievement.'[1] But best of all was a note from the composer:

Monday [30th September 1918]

Dear Adrian

I have discovered that there is no need for me to thank you or to congratulate you. It would be as ridiculous as for you to tell the Queen's Hall orchestra that you didn't know the scores!

You covered yourself with glory and the players are tremendously impressed so is Henry J and your success is so certain that anything I could say or write would be impertinent.

Bless you!
Yr
Gustav

The Planets was put down for public performance in one of Boult's forthcoming Philharmonic concerts – but not complete, as he explained to the composer's friend Vally Lasker.

34 Dover St W.1
17/11/18

Dear Miss Lasker,

Thank you so much for your kind & sympathetic letter. I am always delighted to get helpful suggestions from musicians – particularly when those musicians are on such intimate terms with any work I am undertaking.

Gustav told he he would like to have all 7 planets done at the first performance, & of course there is no question that it would be best for *musicians*, but the general public is a different matter, & I do most strongly feel that when they are being given a totally new language like that, 30 minutes of it is as much as they can take in, & I am quite sure that 90% if not 95% of people only listen to one *moment* after another, & never think of music as a whole at all. I will certainly speak to

[1] *My life of music*, p. 322.

O'Neill again about it – & I need not tell you where my own personal inclinations are in the matter, but I am very much afraid that the practical side of it that I have dwelt on in this letter (in fact, the same point of view that made me cut the Vaughan Williams [*London Symphony*] the second time I did it) is the right one. I will let you know if O'Neill thinks any other arrangement might be made in the programme.

Might I have the scores again some time please (Can I fetch them fr St.P[aul's School] or anywhere)? I should like to 'soak' them properly this time!

With kind regards

> Yrs sincerely
> Adrian C. Boult

From the Mediterranean Holst sent his own suggestions for details in the forthcoming Philharmonic performance of *The Planets*.

Y.M.C.A.
On active service with the British Expeditionary Force
Nov 14 [1918]

Dear Adrian

We are stranded here waiting for a boat. 'Here' being an out-of-the-way little port in South Italy where we get English papers 10 days old. I believe the censorship still holds good so I won't mention its name.

I want to try and collect all my ideas for Jan 30[1] into this letter. Probably you will get postcards containing all the things I forget now.

1) Mars. You made it wonderfully clear – in fact *everything* came out clearly that wonderful morning.

Now could you make more *row*? And work up more sense of climax? Perhaps hurry certain bits? Anyhow it must sound more unpleasant and far more terrifying.

In the middle 5/2 make a lot of $<\quad>$. In the last 5/2 in the 2nd bar the brass have to shorten the last note of the first

---

[1] The date for this first public performance (omitting Nos. 2 and 7) was later postponed to 27th February 1919.

phrase (F in treble and bass) in order to take breath. The organ chord should also have been shortened – it was careless of me to have made it a minim. Would you make it a crochet followed by a crotchet rest so that the organ and brass finish the phrase more or less together?

Whenever there are semiquavers it *might* be well to pull back a little so that they come out clearly and heavily but I leave this to you to decide. The end must be louder and heavier with much more *rall*.

2) Mercury. The part I wanted to alter is when the strings have

or something of the sort. I have arranged it very clumsily between the instruments. It sounds quite well later on the wind and my first idea was to put in on the latter every time. But I am now wishing that I could rearrange the string parts better. Would you? Or you and Norman. The cellos in particular were out of the picture. I forget if they are muted each time it occurs I hope they are. (If this is too much bother leave it as it is) Otherwise Mercury might be all right. Keep him soft and quick.

3) Saturn. In the opening some instruments are quite dead. Others have $<\quad>$. Make the latter as emotional as possible. You got the quicker time just right – all that part goes all right.

The 4 flute tune (Tempo I) was soft enough but try and get the timp, harps and basses also down to nothing. This part must begin from another world and gradually overwhelm this one. That is the nearest verbal suggestion I can give you. Of course there is nothing in any of the planets (*my* planets I mean) that can be expressed in words.

Make the climax as big and overwhelming as possible. Then the soft ending will play itself as long as there is no suggestion of crescendo.

The organ must be softer. It dominated all instead of merely adding depth. Use fewer and softer stops – perhaps 32 ft alone or 16 ft alone instead of both. Let it be too soft rather than too loud.

4) Jupiter. As long as he gets the wonderful joyousness you gave him he'll do. I wish you had Gyp as 1st trumpet!

At the recapitulation this part (tutti in unison)

did not come out clearly. Perhaps it should be broadened out. Do as you like.

And accept my blessing and thanks.

I have been writing this while serving at the canteen with intervals for playing to the men. We have about 60 British sailors here also this place has been inundated with 300 Serbian refugees. They are dear people, far nicer than these natives but there is not enough food for us all in the town. Also they – like us – are taking the first boat to Salonica. It will be certainly overcrowded and probably filthy and there is a gale blowing! However I presume that there will be more than one first boat.

This evening was most interesting. One of the Serbians was a musician. He got a piece of YMCA paper like this one and ruled some lines and wrote out the Serbian national anthem and two dances for me and I played them and they all sang.

Letters will be very welcome

Address G. T. Holst
        c/o C W Bates
        YMCA
        Piccadilly Circus
        Salonica.
                yrs ever
                Gustav

Even then the young conductor had written to ask whether Sir Henry Wood might undertake to give him some lessons. After some delay came a generous answer.

Prince's Hotel, Brighton.
November 18th 1918

Dear Mr. Boult

I don't know what you will think of me, for not replying to your kind note until now, but you know that since the last week of the Promenades, I have not been very well, & have spent most of the days that I have not had a Concert, in bed, resting. That, & my three weeks stay down here, has put me right, & I now feel as fresh & fit as ever.

As regards the Conducting lessons, how can you teach Conducting except with an Orchestra in front of you, to play on. I was *delighted with your direction* of the Van Holst [sic] work, all you want is opportunity, & that will come to you, now that the war is over. If I can be of any assistance to you, over any knotty points, in the direction of Choral or Orchestral works, just send me a line, & we can always arrange a meeting – but a course of lessons – No! No! No! certainly not – ridiculous.

Sincerely yours
Henry J. Wood

With the Philharmonic concert in view, Boult approached Landon Ronald again, but in different terms. Ronald was the dedicatee of Elgar's *Falstaff*, which had been little performed since its premiere in 1913. Ronald was also conducting concerts in the Philharmonic season, and Boult said that if Ronald did not include *Falstaff* he himself would do so. The point was taken, and *Falstaff* was included in Ronald's Philharmonic programme for 5th December 1918. The full score was not yet available from the publishers: it had been engraved in Germany just before the outbreak of war in 1914. Elgar wrote from his cottage in Sussex:

Brinkwells, Fittleworth, Sussex.
Nov 21:1918

My dear Mr Boult:

I have been asking Messrs Novello about *Falstaff*: the full sc: will be published shortly. I fear there are to be some 'pen'

37

corrections – the f.sc. was engraved in Germany & very much hurried I fear

> With very kind regards
> Yours sincerely
> Edward Elgar

Learning of Elgar's newly completed Sonata for violin and piano, Adrian Boult tried to secure the first performance for the new British Music Society. And he heard of Elgar's candidacy for his own Club, the Savile.

Brinkwells, Fittleworth, Sussex.
Nov 24 1918

My dear Mr. Boult:
Our letters crossed. thanks for yours & for 'aiding & abetting' at the Savile.

I am sorry I cannot say anything about the Sonata – it is not yet completely engraved &, as things are so slow, I have no idea as to its appearance in print. I fear I cannot let the B. Music Socy have the *first* performance.

I hope you will be able to get *Falstaff* before the Philharmonic Concert.

> Kindest rgds
> Yours sincy
> Edward Elgar

Boult attended both the concert and the rehearsal which preceded it.

One important composer whose work had not been represented in the London Symphony series was Delius. So Adrian Boult was invited to conduct the premiere performance of Delius's Violin Concerto for the first of his two Philharmonic concerts on 30th January 1919. The soloist was the Concerto's dedicatee, Albert Sammons. Afterwards he sent a letter to the composer, and received this reply:

44 Belsize Park Gardens NW 3.
Wednesday [5 Feb. 1919]

Dear Mr Boult
Many thanks for your letter: Since the Concert I have been

confined to the house with a cold (not influenza) but am almost well again.

Do come up & have tea with us one afternoon – say at 3-30–4? the changes of tempo can easily be marked in the score

The Concerto received quite a wonderful reception, most gratifying to me & I should like to thank you again for the care & sympathy you gave to the work – What a pity the Philharmonic can not repeat it during the season; We might then attain a quite perfect performance – I suppose a repetition is impossible! Sammons was splendid –

Do come & we will have a talk about things musical in London –

Sincerely yours
Frederick Delius

Tel 879 Hampstead

After the Philharmonic performance of *The Planets* on 27th February, Boult sent a cable of congratulations to Holst in Salonika.

YMCA British Post Office Constantinople
March 25 [1919]

Dear Adrian

It was very a) nice of you

b) like you to send that cable. Many many thanks for it. Unfortunately I only arrived here three days ago and nobody troubled to send the wire on to me.

And now a mail is in and I have learnt details. And the chief detail I have learnt – if one can call it a detail – is your triumphant success. You saw the papers long before I did so I won't quote them. But you seem to have won the hearts of my young lady pupils very thoroughly also those of others who are neither young nor ladies. 'I must tell you how beautifully Mr Boult conducted. One hardly noticed him at all but from the way things went one realized how masterly he was.' That is real deep praise from a discerning musician. 'Boult was absolutely glorious.' 'The performance was beautiful, Boult took immense trouble and conducted finely.' Etc. etc.

So it is good to know that you have reaped your reward and that other people have expressed the gratitude that I can only feel.

I had all my kit stolen the other day so do not know your address. I shall therefore enclose it in the next letter I write to my wife or Miss Lasker.

Yrs Ever
Wishing you much more of the same success and myself also
Gustav

The Abbey Manor, West Kirby, Cheshire.
or 6 Chelsea Court SW. 3.
20/4/19.

Dear Gustav,

Thank you so much for your very jolly letter, but don't you see that none of the nice things you & your friends have said would have been possible if YOU hadn't made them so?

It was *sickening* that you weren't there to see the enthusiasm & to be the butt of it! I hear that it may be possible for the R.P.S. to repeat the Planets next season – I don't know who will conduct – but it would be splendid to hear it, & splendid to do it again. It was gorgeous the way it all came off, & the way the orchestra loved it, & how well people spoke of it afterwards.

By the bye we shortened the organ glissando – starting at

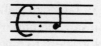

because otherwise the notes had hardly time to speak. As it was I only heard the last note, but think the *feel* of it came through to the audience.

All blessings, & hoping we'll have them all again soon

Yrs ever
Adrian

How *maddening* about your kit.

When the full score of *The Planets* was published in 1921, Holst inscribed a copy:

This score is the property of Adrian Boult who first caused the Planets to shine in public and so earned the gratitude of Gustav Holst.

At last, with the war over, Boult could take the Mus.Doc. degree for which he had passed the examination at Oxford in 1914. He was to be twitted about this when he took over the orchestra of Diaghilev's Russian Ballet at short notice in the autumn of 1919; the writer was Sir Henry Wood.

Langham Hotel, London.
October 5th. 1919

My dear Mr. Boult

Do accept my *very sincerest congratulations*, on your Conducting of 'Russian Ballet' in London – this settles it, you can never be a Doctor of Music after this, can you. Please send me a post card of the date of the first Matinée of DeFalla's Ballet, I can only attend Matinées, & I missed it, at the Alhambra.

With all good wishes.
Sincerely yours
Henry J. Wood

P.S. I am back home again for six months, 4 Elsworthy Road, N.W.

After the *Three-cornered hat* performances, Boult received a visit from Edward Dent's friend J. B. Trend (later Professor of Spanish at Cambridge), who told him about Falla's *Nights in the Gardens of Spain* and put him in touch with the composer.

66 Ave Mozart, Paris XVI[e]
2. 1. 920

Dear Sir,[1]

It is a great pleasure to receive your letter and to accept your very kind invitation to luncheon next Sunday at 1 p.m. in the Palais d'Orsay.

We will talk over the subject of the Nocturnes about which

[1] Translated from French.

Mr Trend has spoken to you, and I shall look forward to thanking you personally for your conducting in the performances of my ballet in London.

In the meantime please accept, dear sir, my best wishes.

Manuel de Falla

Concert-room activities also went forward. For a London Symphony concert to introduce the violinist Samuel Dushkin in March 1920, Boult decided to include Elgar's Second Symphony (which, like *Falstaff*, had been given few performances since its premiere). On 11th February he went to Severn House to go through the score with Elgar, who came with his daughter Carice to the rehearsal on 15th March.

Monday evg [15th March 1920]

My dear Adrian:

I was so very sorry to have to rush away without thanking you properly for your kindness & artistic care of my work: you do it spendidly – don't be afraid to let the first movement go & the Celli in the opening of the finale might play *out free* almost – *mf*.

But all was splendid & exactly right. Bless you & thank you

Yours v sincy
Edward Elgar

Of the concert at Queen's Hall the following evening, Lady Elgar was an eloquent witness.

Wonderful performance of the Symphony. From beginning to end it seemed absolutely to penetrate the audience's mind & heart. After 1st movement great applause & *shouts*, rarely heard till end, & great applause all through. Adrian was wonderful – At end frantic enthusiasm & they dragged out E. who looked very overcome, hand in hand with Adrian at least 3 times. E. was so happy & pleased.

Severn House Hampstead, N.W.
March 17 1920

My dear Adrian: With the sounds ringing in my ears I send a word of thanks for your splendid conducting of the Sym: – I am most grateful to you for your affectionate care of it & I feel that my reputation in the future is safe in your hands. It was a wonderful series of sounds. Bless you!

        Yours very snly
        Edward Elgar

The 'Boys' *will* take very long bows when the thing flows violin-wise – I wish we cd. mark the parts as some old fiddle books were with a bow & pricks shewing the *part* of the bow to be used   thus.

Severn House Hampstead, N.W.3.
17 March 1920.

Dear Mr. Adrian Boult

    I must send you a few lines to thank you from my heart for your wonderful performance last evening. I cannot describe the delight to me of hearing that great work so splendidly rendered. You made it so clear & irresistible that I feel sure it penetrated straight to the minds & hearts of numbers who had failed to understand it – I rejoiced in your triumph & hope it will be succeeded by every possible success for you – I only hope you are not quite exhausted by the tremendous demands of the work. I know you will like to hear that Edward was *so* happy & delighted it has done him so much good –

    Thank you –

    Yours very sincerely

        C. A. Elgar

Another member of the audience that night was John Ireland.

14A, Gunter Grove, Chelsea, S.W.10
March:17 1920

My dear Boult

    I was deeply moved by yr. splendid performance of Elgar's truly noble Symphony: it was a great event, & will, I hope, do much to clear the air. We owe you so much for so clearly demonstrating that the greatest music of the present time is by a Briton & that a British conductor with a British orchestra can rise to such heights of Art in interpretation.

I did not wait to hear the other works – as I felt Elgar & yourself had already given me enough to think about.

Yrs sincerely

John Ireland:

For Lady Elgar it was almost a last hearing of her husband's music. She was already ill, and on 7th April she died. It was, as all their close friends recognised, the end of Elgar's creative life.

The Abbey Manor, West Kirby, Cheshire.

11th April 1920

Dear Sir Edward –

I only got back yesterday from Holland – with Arthur Bliss & some other pupils & it was a terrible shock to us all to see the very sad announcement from Severn House when we opened the *Telegraph* at Harwich.

How much more terrible it must be for you it is impossible for us to realise – but no one could fail to see how much more than a perfect union was there in Severn House.

Lady Elgar wrote me an extraordinarily kind letter after the concert the other day, & this will be a treasured possession all my life.

It is impossible for one who has not so suffered to know the meaning of such a bereavement as yours – but one can sympathise, & that surely all are doing who have ever known her, or you, or who have come under the spell of your music.

In all sympathy,

Yours very sincerely

Adrian C. Boult.

Writing again in August, Elgar sent his reply to the final point in Boult's letter. But he was also looking to the future through his hopes for the younger man's career. He nominated him for The Athenaeum, and looked at the chance of his admission under Rule II which provides for 'the annual introduction of a certain number of persons of distinguished eminence in science, literature or the arts, or for their public services . . .'

Brinkwells, Fittleworth, Sussex
Augt 5 1920

My dear Adrian Boult:

I had the pleasure to put your name in the Ath: proposal book: I will ask [Hugh] Allen to second you & am writing to him in a post or two – this will give you time to send him a line also so that the letters may arrive somewhere about the same time; – I expect he is far away just now. As to the Ath: – I hope in time you may be invited to join under Rule II – this is really a great honour – if, however, your election in the ordy way should come on you can always withdraw if you like, so you are committed to nothing: in any case I have had the joy & satisfaction of proposing you.

I am lonely now & do not see music in the old way & cannot believe I shall *complete* any new work – sketches I still make but there is no inducement to finish anything; – ambition I have none; many thanks for thinking of performing anything: it is wonderful to see how you have 'developed' & the greatest satisfaction to one who believed in your ability from the first.

Best regards Yours sincy
Edward Elgar

Boult's reply sent news of a prospective tour of Prague – where he decided to repeat Elgar's Second Symphony – Vienna, and Munich, together with a brace of grouse from his father's shooting.

Fittleworth
Aug 22 1920

My dear Adrian:

Many thanks for the birds which arrived yesterday; it is most kind of you to send them. I am glad you are extending your tour in Germany & I shall be grateful if you will give my warm greetings to Strauss: it is difficult to know how feelings have stood the wear & strain of the last few years, it may be, that S. will not be too 'receptive', anyhow it will be kind to *me* if you can assure him of my continued admiration &, if he will, friendship. I have followed, as well as broken communications could allow, his later compositions; I cannot expect him to be interested in mine – he has probably forgotten the good old days when he was named (by me) Richard Coeur de Lion, but I hope not. I know *nothing* of Prague & fully expect the whole thing has fallen through: I believe Lalla [Vandevelde] is going to Tiflis, etc. etc. & will be away a long time. I had the pleasure to see her at Ridgehurst three weeks ago* & she left for Brussels: so all is chaos as far as I am concerned: to tell the truth I never understood what she had to do with the affair, so my ignorance, although deep, is not sudden.

I hope you are having good weather

Best regards,
Yours sincy
Edward Elgar

* of course, we lunched with you during that time at R.
P.S. – I kept your note of Augt 8 – it is kind of you to think of new compositions but I cannot bear the thought of music. Thank you for putting down *Cockaigne*.

Boult was to conduct his first performance of Elgar's *Cockaigne* Overture with the London Symphony Orchestra at the Palladium on 28th November.

Then another London orchestra appeared. It was the British Symphony Orchestra, formed by returning servicemen, and Adrian Boult had taken over its direction. A series of concerts was presented at the Kingsway Hall, and on the programme for 20th November Boult put down the Elgar Second Symphony for another performance.

Severn House Hampstead, N.W.
Nov 9 1920

My dear Adrian:
Very many thanks for your letter: I hope to be able to come to the rehearsal, to which you kindly invite me, on Saturday morning, the 20th. at Kingsway Hall. It will be lovely to hear you do the Symphony again.

Carice & I are trying to start life again here, but (you will easily understand) it is sad, sad work to gather up the threads.

I hope you will come & see us soon: I am just off to Birmingham – on my return we will try to fix something

> Best regards
> Yours very sincerely
> Edward Elgar

Saturday evening [20th November 1920]

My dear Adrian:

I am so woefully sorry but I had to go straight home & lie down – not as a consequence of the rehearsal but a miserable recurrence of very painful neuralgia. Alas! – I was delighted with the 'making' of your orchestra and the attention & interest of the members was first class – a fine band of men

Good luck to them

> My love to you
> Yours ever
> Edward Elgar

Meanwhile Boult had accepted a distinguished academic appointment in London. Following the death of Parry in October 1918, Hugh Allen became Director of the Royal College of Music. One of his first acts was to invite Adrian Boult to start a conducting class on the lines of the Leipzig Conservatory. The class had begun in February 1919, and soon accounts of it were appearing in the press. Katherine Eggar reported for *The Music Student*:[1]

To see something of the actual working of this new departure in British Musical Education is of course of enormous interest, and it was the present writer's pleasant privilege to spend the greater part of a recent Wednesday at the R.C.M., watching Mr. Boult's students under instruction.

They have a five-class day. The first half of the morning is given to actual conducting, the second half to being conducted, that is to say, to singing in the Choral Class under the Director's bâton. The afternoon starts with an hour of score-playing; next comes an hour of criticism of the morning's

[1] *The Music Student*, January 1921, pp. 220–1.

47

conducting, and lastly an hour devoted to the study of some particular concerto or symphony in theory.

'We try to give our conductors every conceivable difficulty in the way of conditions,' explained Mr. Boult, as we stood waiting for a little orchestra to assemble in the middle of the huge empty Hall of the R.C.M. 'We provide them with a scratch collection of players, the most inexperienced in College; they have to do without a good many of the essentials (for instance, I'm just going to start them rehearsing a Bach suite for flute without any flute); this Hall when half empty is more impossibly difficult in the way of sound than any place I know, and you notice that I have the piano placed right away from the orchestra, behind them, upon the platform. I've got Harold Samuel coming to play the Bach D minor presently. Of course Concertos are far the best practice for the young conductor – it's so much easier just to keep the band going than to grasp the soloist's wishes and brush them instantly on to the orchestra. No, the erection this side of the conductor's desk is not a gibbet where we exact the death penalty from incompetent conductors; its something to do with the opera theatre which is being constructed in the basement. You'll hear the hammering presently – just another of the little difficulties that add piquancy to our conducting struggles. And, by the bye, you've come on a record day for 'conditions'; the boiler of the heating apparatus has chosen this nice cold, foggy morning *to burst*, and I'm afraid you'll have a chilly time sitting here listening to our struggles, which I must now go and start.'

He moved away, and in a few moments a student was in the conductor's desk collecting the attention of his shivering players. There was no chilliness in the mental atmosphere, however, and the task of directing an incoordinate assembly of inexperienced readers is not one which leaves, at any rate, the conductor cold. So as conductor succeeded conductor, and the Concerto followed the Suite, there was a general *crescendo* of animation to which the presence of the distinguished soloist added not a little. Mr. Boult meantime moved about the Hall smiling, helpful, observant, un-fussy, now and

48

then jotting down the notes which in the afternoon would reveal the shortcomings of the novices, and the Visitor was free to gather impressions.

The chief feature is a sort of gay earnestness. There is no relentless pounding through in spite of bewilderment. When it is better to stop and start again, this is done. When the conductor is in desperate straits, Mr. Boult is at his elbow with a word of enlightenment. . . .

Then at last, the end of the Concerto being reached, the company pull themselves together for a final non-stop run through the first movement. The conductors gather round the desk, and at a sign from Mr. Boult, one of them mounts it and raises the stick. The pianist's eye and his meet, and off they go. Presently Mr. Samuel glances up again, and it is clear from his expression that he has had a shock which would have unnerved a less experienced player. 'Surely,' he says to the piano as his fingers fly over the keys, 'it was a tall boy with a pale face who was conducting when I started, but just now I could swear it was a girl moving the stick. I'll make sure at the end of this run. . . . Heavens! it's somebody with a moustache. . . . Well, I'm blowed, if I didn't see a shock of red hair this time. . . . No, it's a bald head . . . no, he's got a black mop . . . well, here we are in at the death together anyhow.'

By this time, at the back of the hall, students of all subjects were collecting for the Choral Class, and a few minutes later the platform was packed with them. In the absence, through indisposition, of the Director, Mr. Boult presided, and took the Class through a new work by a former Collegian and part of the Beethoven Mass.

After luncheon, the Conductors assembled in a class room with two pianos, for score-playing. A Minuet and Rondo from a Haydn Symphony, parts of *Manfred*, of the *Mastersingers*, of the Brahms C minor Symphony, kept pairs of players busy for an hour, one player taking strings and the other wind, and changing rôles at the word of command. Mr. Boult made brief comments and interpolated words of advice as the music progressed, and then at three o'clock came the Day of Judg-

49

ment. We all settled down to hear our condemnation, and the Recording Angel opened the book.

'Brown, your *rehearsing* was really excellent. You show them how. But you had no control at change of time. Now why was that? . . . *You stopped the stick between the beats*. You see, your too definite beat stopped the swing. You had got to arm's length and had left yourself nowhere to go. The definite beat is all very well if everybody sees it, but you've got to contend with the player who looks up *between* the beats. Remember page 17, last paragraph, in our famous book. [A Handbook on the *Technique of Conducting.*]

'Green, you and the band couldn't agree; you remember the place. You must count out loud if you can't get them with you.' 'But I did.' 'Yes – but they couldn't hear you. You must bellow if necessary.'

'Black, you were put out because the desk was too high. If you find yourself in that difficulty it does not solve the problem to conduct from the trouser pocket as you were doing. The players *must* see your stick. Now the height of the desk is a most important point, both for your own ease in moving the arm and also for the view of the players, especially in opera conducting when the hall is in darkness and the orchestra only sees the point of the stick by the light thrown up from the conductor's desk. You must ask the players where they can see your stick and then put your desk just below that.'

'Miss Grey, where do you beat the "and" in six-time? . . . and those grace notes . . . ? Well, I think it would be worth while to stop and discuss grace-notes' (so we did) . . . 'And, White, you got into difficulties in the last movement and looked very fierce – not that that mattered, but why didn't you *do* something?' 'Well, I was furious with them for not doing what I wanted, but I didn't like to pull them up. I mean, you don't feel you can waste the time of a man like Harold Samuel while you pitch into people.' 'O, he wouldn't have minded your stopping him, and you must practise everything, bullying included, you know!'

50

'Now, everybody, please – the second fiddles were still badly left out.' General murmur of guiltiness.

'And then about getting into touch with your soloist; your eyes *must* meet over the starts and finishes. And remember, it's no good to get ready with him and then collect the orchestra. It's the other way about. "Are *you* (the orchestra) ready?" Then leave them, fix the soloist, and act with him. Yes, Scarlett, what were you going to say?'

'I got into a mess over the change of beat. I'm afraid it would have been very obvious in a performance. But what happens, Sir, when you're conducting a professional orchestra and you miss a beat? Will they do what you show, or will they do it right?'

'O, the professional orchestra will carry their conductor over a misbeat; they'll save you from a catastrophe, unless it happens that you've ruffled them beforehand. Of course, if you've got the wrong side of them at rehearsal, they'll take the greatest pains to follow your mis-directions exactly! But talking of misbeats, did you notice what happened at the concert on Saturday?' Here followed thrilling details of recent experiences, hints as to possible traps at performance, suggestions for emergencies, reminiscences of various soloists' idiosyncracies in particular works; and then the clock struck four, time for the last class.

Liszt's Concerto in E♭ was the work chosen for detailed study during this hour, a work which contains more pitfalls for the unwary conductor, Mr. Boult considers, than almost any other piano Concerto.

And so to the day's end.

Teaching at the College brought contacts with another range of distinguished personalities. One of the piano teachers was Fanny Davies, the most distinguished English pupil of Clara Schumann. Organ was taught by Sir Waltcr Parratt, the Master of the King's Musick and organist of St. George's Chapel, Windsor. The College orchestra was conducted by Sir Charles Stanford, and Boult was to act as his assistant. At one moment that brought a small friction, as shown in this letter from an old friend who was a member of the College Council, Robert Finnie McEwen.

Marchmont, Berwickshire.
Friday.

My dear Boult, Your kind letter delights me. I am sure
W[alter] P[arratt] would be immensely pleased and gratified.
It is really so pathetic to see him and C.V.S., like two old stags,
feeling a bit displaced by the splendid vigour of you younger
ones! There's no stupid resentment on their part. They are all
as proud as Punch of you and their young colleagues at
College, and all your achievements they are never tired of
extolling. And yet there is just that claim for a place in the sun
themselves, which you all would be the very last to deny them.
It makes them a little bit inclined to be suspicious of innocent
actions which ought not to give rise to any misapprehension
on their part. But you've done just the right thing – and it is so
nice of you to say you did not regard what I told you as in any
way an unwarrantable liberty to take. 1,000 thanks!

. . . Ever yours,
R. F. McEwen

Another letter came from H. C. Colles, who lectured on the
history of music at the College and wrote reviews of College concerts – not always to Sir Charles Stanford's delight. On this occasion
he was dodging the post-war enthusiasm of Rosa Newmarch and
Fanny Davies for Czechoslovak music.

42 Orsett Terrace, W.2.
Feb 26. 1920.

My dear Boult
    I have a confession to make. You evidently do not realize
the depths of turpitude to which the hunted animal may
fall. Some time ago, long before our walk across the park, Mrs
R. N. announced that she was coming to lunch and wanted 'a
little talk' with me afterwards. I feared the worst and fears
were confirmed when the talk turned gradually from her
interesting experiences in Czecho-Slovakia to the formation
of a C-S Committee in London. I talked nervously of the
advantages of small committees; I declared that three was the
ideal number (I knew she already had two members besides

52

herself), but there was no escape. At last in despair I offered another life and saved my own. I said how nice you were and how interested I thought you would be. With mingled joy and shame I saw that for the moment I was saved. I heard no more of Czecho-Slovakia until this morning's post brought your cry for help! Then my conscience smote me.

After this I shall not be surprized if when we meet you pass me by with a stony Stanfordian stare, the sort of stare I get the morning *after* an RCM concert (the morning before is generally all smiles).

If however you still want me and I can be of any use I will try to expiate my sin that way.

Of course I love both Mrs R.N. and Miss F.D.; it's committees I hate!

Yours ever
H. C. Colles.

And then a request for help over the Schumann tradition brought this voluble response from Fanny Davies:

2, Holland Lane, Melbury Road, Kensington, W.
[n.d.]

Dear Mr. Boult,

Of course I will.

I think it *so* necessary to try one's level best to get the right traditions (I don't mean just hearsay – but great traditions such as those that go down & down & make our Navy) put into the conductor's work. I should very much like a talk with you on this subject

Hurrying ends is the *great* drawback to our orchestras – they make for 'line' – but they get to the end too soon, so the soloist has to hurry.

The *Schumann* Concerto is of course the one I have very much at heart & would come & play it & *talk it* to them – *any* time you like that *I* can – e.g. the dragging of the 1st clarinet theme – often as the clarinet was playing at his own funeral – & all detached. The hurrying of the beautiful 2nd theme & the triplet passages in piano – off they go! – new gear! & leave the

53

beautiful things on the way, to be *lost* to view. The *awful* cut up-ness of the fugal bit in the last movement – & the heavy, or *marionette*-like playing of the wonderful 'wingy' second

theme of the last movement – My mind 'schweben' but nearly always it is made into a coy, smart, sniffy staccato nip. If they knew how much beauty they lose, when conducting it so, & not *insisting* on the *poetry* being brought out – they surely wouldn't do it? Just the same at the Prom on Thursday & poor old Borwick going his way when he could poor lamb!! But I have heard it worse than that. All the 'drilling' in the world is to me naught, if I can't get a bit of real soul into an orchestra – even if it's out of tune; cold perfection is terrible –

Another is the Emperor. Very important.

Another is the *Bach D minor* with string *accompt* Will you oblige me very much & let Margaret Hayes play this with *you* – it is quite ready & *ought to come on at an informal concert*. I have the parts (proper bowings) marked – or rather eliminated – all the *fleas* taken away! The phrasing of that in the parts is so clearly – hop-hop-hop – & all in wrong place. Oh! *do* lets have a talk on the piano, just you & me I mean –

I'd like to discuss lots of symphony bits too – hundreds of things – that can be made great – *or very small* – Elasticity too & *space*.

I should very much like to play the Bach D minor with them (*you* I mean!) That 2nd movement, & the *dry* cut, treatment more than often, of the appoggiatura – They seem to forget that there is such a thing as Vorschlag – which makes it thus

– then it has a meaning – & not only that, it makes the piano parts *match* it – otherwise they are discordant often, & not Bachisch at all.

But the pedants who go by 'one rule for one & all grace notes' (therefore making them *un*grace notes) – invariably have the short note *on* the beat unless it be ♪ & the real musical sense – comes in too late!! I remember how Joachim treated Vorschläge, don't you! just *dropping them* in – neither with nor not 'with' e.g. in that amazing obbligato in the S. Matthew

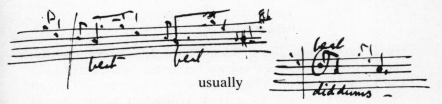

usually

& very *stiff* sounding of course.

Then . . . the tempo of the C major Schubert – under Richter – & under Snukes. . . . The Scherzo of more than one Schumann Symphony – Yes & I'll do the S. Let these be *my* concertos so far!!! I'll make it do on a Wed: Klein had no business to play the Schumann at all yet! She can't play it for nuts – but she has worked with a pupil of mine (Edie Barnett not in the College for help – at technique –) in the holidays & at last I believe we've got lightness coming. *Slow* Clementi Gradus 5 fingers. Isn't it amazing.

Yours very sincerely
Fanny Davies

I want *Robertson* to do the Emperor – it *is* ready for rehearsal. *Soon!* & good.

Outside the College, activities continued in full cry. Elgar had recently returned from a short tour in Amsterdam and Brussels. Boult followed him in April 1921, and sent news of Cornelis Dopper, the Dutch composer and assistant conductor of the Concertgebouw Orchestra. And there was a plan to produce a performance of Elgar's Violin Concerto at the People's Palace with the young violinist Frederick Holding, in the autumn.

Severn House, 42, Netherhall Gardens, Hampstead, N.W.
Ap 19 1921

My dear Adrian: Many thanks for your news of Mr Dopper – I cannot understand the loss of the letters.

I shall be delighted to hear Mr. Holding play the Concerto & hope he may have a chance to do it with you & your orch: – he might ring up anytime & find if I am available, *but* I am giving up everything & arranging to depart quietly as soon as things can be conveniently managed.

My love & good wishes to you
Yours very sincerely
Edward Elgar

Elgar was shortly to give up Severn House, Hampstead, where his important works had been written during the last years of Lady Elgar's life. He was in no happy mood for a Promenade Concert which included his Violin Concerto and *Falstaff* at Queen's Hall on 1st September. Their old friend Frank Schuster (the dedicatee of *In the South*) had rushed back from a continental sojourn which included Pfitzner's opera *Palestrina* especially to be present, as he wrote to Boult afterwards.

White's
3 September [1921]

Dear Adrian

It was good to have news of you on my return. – & such a return! The journey – though lengthy, was nothing compared to the trouble fume & fret of getting my luggage through the customs at Brussels. For some unknown reason it did *not* travel by the same train, & was nowhere to be found at Herbesthal. I wanted to remain there & *wait* for it (wisely I

56

think) but was dissuaded from it by the *chef de douane* who promised to send it on by next train. Yes – *but* oh my dear! from 8 am to *10 am* I was hunting it in Brussels all over the interminable town & *stations* & only pulled it through by the skin of my teeth in time to start with it at 10.8, and reach Queen's Hall in the middle of the 1st movement of the concerto (well but quite *incredibly* played by Tessie whats her name[1]) – The Falstaff *sounded* to me all right if not especially brilliant, but Ronald – whom I met this morning – thought otherwise (which means little after all) Edward had a tremendous reception (– perhaps bigger *before* than *after* it?) & took his calls with that appearance of sulkiness which would *do* for any composer of less commanding genius. I could have slapped him (& very nearly did) when I went round to tell him what I had done & encountered to be present & was greeted with the *coldest* of hand shakes! –

Palestrina ????????? Well – intensely boring until suddenly – I don't quite know why – it *grips* one & won't let one go. I went again (for 2 acts) & find that it is perhaps a certain *sincerity* and austerity which does the trick – anyway it is individual & something quite *new* as regards subject & treatment. It is the most marvellous piece of *management* and *performance* I ever saw. 'Don Giovanni' was *very nearly bad* & 'Iphigenia' deadly dull, in spite of a glorious performance – the orchestra strings in the overture of overwhelming *majesty!*

> Anzie's love.
> Your affece.
> Frank

Elgar's interest had been stirred a little by a luncheon with Richard Strauss, at which Adrian Boult had been present. They discussed the orchestration of Bach's organ music, and Strauss promised to transcribe the Fantasia in C minor. Elgar made an elaborate transcription of the Fugue. He wrote from Hereford, where he was staying for the Three Choirs Festival.

[1] Margaret Fairless.

57

Brockhampton Court, Hereford.
Sep 3 1921

My dear Adrian: I think you may be back from Munich – send me word here about your concert plans. I have the last proof of the fugue & many are anxious to give it a hearing – when are your dates etc.

I wish you were here – lovely country.

> Best regards
> Yours ever sincy
> Edward Elgar

Unfortunately the dates did not fit, and the Fugue transcription's premiere went to Eugene Goossens.

Brockhampton Court, Hereford.
Thursday Sep 8 1921

My dear Adrian:

Forgive a very hasty note – I am the midst of a whirlwind: – I am so very sorry but I fear the *fugue* must appear a little earlier than you can manage. The thing is not worth any fuss – only I shd have been delighted if you had done it first

> Frantic haste
> Ever yours
> Edward Elgar

But Elgar did attend the Violin Concerto performance with Frederick Holding on 13th November.

37 St J[ame]s's Place SW1
Tuesday [15th November 1921]

My dear Adrian:

I have been so rushed that I cd. not send a note before: I had to rush away in the fog before the end of the Mozart or I shd. have come round to you & Mr. Holding to thank you for the performance of the Concerto – the orchestra was fine & flawless. Mr. Holding did well but hid an artistic nervousness

58

which made him hurry sometimes in the 'passages' – but it was good & will you thank him from me for his playing?

> Best regards
> Ever yours
> Edward Elgar

On 1st December at the People's Palace Boult conducted another performance of the Second Symphony which pleased Elgar more than the earlier one. Meanwhile Boult was preparing his first appearance with orchestras on the continent. He received this letter from Arthur Bliss, with whom he had shared experiences at the Royal College of Music and a trip to Germany. Bliss was working on the score of his ballet *Mêlée fantasque.*

21 Holland Park W.11
Tuesday evening

My dear Adrian.

It was good to get your letter and the lecture which indeed reached me at a lucky moment. I had just reached the 50th page of the *Mêlée* score – since seeing you I have recast a great deal of it in a more serious vein, due mainly to the fact that the time for passing from the experimentalizing to the realizing has almost come. I am very proud of it, and do hope you will like it on the 13th. I should much like to show you the score first measuring as it does some 2 feet by 1½, – because it has been written largely from a conducting point of view – there are so many things that I hear in it, which may fail as in Clark's case the hand cannot accompany the brain right to the most subtle point. I should be so overjoyed if it could go to Prague with you, as I know you are the man for it – bar joking.

Now about Vienna. I am very anxious to do so, – I suggest 3 Concerts in all: – 2 in the big hall, & 1 in the smaller. In the smaller, English Singers, my Chamber Rhapsody & Rout – Myra solos – In the larger hall – two big orchestral programmes, including *Mêlée F*[antasque], & the double Concerto – Those I do not mind whether I conduct or you do – The point is I wish to be a composer there only, and should not dream of conducting any one else's work on that occasion – Please let me know if you think I am grossly overdoing my own work – Noy & the Clarinet Songs will be done in Vienna *twice* this Winter – so they will be able to get ready their hissing –

You see Myra can play other Concertos too with you – as also could any of the English singers in passages from the Beethoven Mass etc. I think it would be really a *most* useful & helpful business & benefit *both of us* in *London* tremendously. I am rather sick of the semi-prevalent idea that I am a brilliant ammer [i.e. amateur] and nothing else. – if only folk knew the amount of work I've put in to the last 3 years to try & advance on the goal of serious music, they would stop this silly sensational chatter.

I am all for Germany on the 13th. I have never been to the Fatherland. I go on to Salzburg again 1st of Sept & will come up to meet you when you like –

1 How do I get a passport?
2 What clothes shall I take?
3 What Scores?
4 Anything else?

Yours as ever
Arthur

Duties at the College continued to be diverse and demanding. A typically brief congratulation came from Sir Charles Stanford following a performance of his Concert variations on 'Down among the dead men', op. 71.

9, Lower Berkeley Street, Portman Square, W.L.
Oct 29, 21

My dear Boult,
It was an admirable performance, & I thank you very much for all the care you gave to it. The whole concert was very good (& I lost my 6d. to HPA)

Yrs very sincerely
C V Stanford

Ethel Smyth, Harold Samuel, and Sir George Henschel all sent their requests and enthusiasm. Miss Smyth pushed her own interests as composer of *The Boatswain's Mate* – not only at the College but at the Old Vic, where she had harassed Lilian Baylis's conductor Charles Corri and now attacked Adrian Boult, for Boult had recently become a governor of the Old Vic.

Coign Woking
Jan. 9th 1922

Dear Mr. Boult. You may wonder why I don't ask Miss Baylis what I am asking you – but she is such a grand optimist, & may be so unaccustomed to such events as playing a *new* opera (new for the Old Vic) from *new* parts & a *newly* bowdlerised score that she'd wonder what I was talking about.

She *did* let out that when Corri is working up to some new performance (like his score of *Tristan*) that he gets in ¼ of an hour here & 15 mins there over a considerable space of time before the day of genuine *Tristan* rehearsal arrives. Alas! I can't do that of course.

Now I am going to write to Sir Hugh to ask if he can help me when it comes to playing through the parts. But even so, *you* know what a ticklish job it would be, even for a very routined conductor, to meet his orchestra for the first time at the Dress Rehearsal. . . .

What I want to know is, is there *no* possibility of an extra *orchestral* rehearsal? If the worst came to the worst & one had to pay for it, have you an idea what it would cost? I don't know how many strings they have there, but otherwise my score wants 9 (4 wood 4 brass & Drums) Indeed if the worst came to the worst I *might* use the Version B. (4 wood 1 Brass 1 drums & solo Strings! 11 people instead of 17 or 18 but that would be a pity.)

I think I was rash to say 'go ahead' without making any stipulation about the rehearsals with orchestra. If they *never do* call an orchestral rehearsal, & never have, of course I can't ask them to. But I am giving them the Pfe Scores myself, having persuaded my publisher to charge nothing for the hire of the orch: material (for which I shd. get half the fee, usually) & also to accept £5 for 3 performances (as royalty) I myself telling him he can keep it all for himself. So I'm doing all I can.

If you will tell me what you think can be done I should be

deeply grateful, for, as musician you see the whole thing.
Please forgive me for bothering you & with best wishes for
1922 I am yours sincerely

　　　　　　Ethel Smyth

What about Vienna?

Harold Samuel looked forward to a two-piano rehearsal of the
Brahms D minor Concerto:

During the summer of 1922 Boult attended operatic performances conducted by Bruno Walter in Munich. And there was
Ethel Smyth again – this time creating a situation for comic opera,
and evidently frightening Bruno Walter with her volubility.

Hotel Nürnbergerhof Karlsbad
13.8.22

My dear Mr. Boult

That I shd. borrow Mk 1000 of you to pay for an opera
ticket – *das geht noch*; but that I shd. ask you to pay a washing
bill for me (specially such a tiny one) . . . *das geht eigentlich
nicht!* But to no less a matter than this has the enclosed 300
Mk reference!!

When I went to Salzburg I left a few garments to be washed
& you know how, after all, I was not to find a bed at the Park.
Thus it came that I forgot all about it till I hit on the duplicate
list in my pocket book . . . which event took place at 10 pm on
Friday night when I was packing to start next morn: at 7.40. *It
was pouring* (as you may remember) and I had my wraps
already at the Station – rather foolishly including my water
proof. So I dared not sally forth again & soak.

The maidservant flew next morning to the Hotel, & like a
brick brought me the *Wäsche* to my train, but there was no bill
therein! – All this I had foreseen also that perhaps there wd.
be no *Wäsche* ready. So I sent by her a note to the Direktor
saying that in this case wd. he forward it by Post & get the
costs out of you – or (if the *Wäsche* ready) to give it to bearer
& (as before) get the costs out of you(!)

As I think these cannot turn out, even in a Hotel, to be
more than Mk 300 I send you, anyhow, that sum; with un-
utterable apologies. Do tell all yr. friends how *very* sorry I was
not to say goodbye to them (specially nice Mr. Clegg,[1] abt.
whom I have remorse! He *does* ask silly, tripping-up questions – I think to gain time – but he has something very golden
about him . . . & *he's a gentleman* – a quality I confess to
greatly appreciating even in quite superficial intercourse!)

[1] Humphrey Proctor-Gregg.

O & will you tell Mr Taylor that I shd be so glad if he'd tell me who is Rosé's agent? I met R. in the Artists Room & . . . we embraced . . . which wd. not surprise you if you had heard them play my 4th! – He *suggested* to me playing some of my instrumental songs in London & I am going tentatively to ask Miss Thursfield if, other things equal, she wd. like the job – (All this en l'air)

I saw Walter; he was in a tearing hurry & I had a distressed feeling that he is no longer the same man (tho' a far better conductor than he was). I think, or rather I know, that the chief reason of his departure is the Jew-baiting that monarchic Bavaria is carrying to all lengths. He is the only one of all my old friends, now re-met for the first time since the war, between whom & myself I felt there was no real warm touch – my friendly attack glided off sham-sunny marble, & I felt all lost with that glittering restless eye & evident preoccupation with God knows what – perhaps a life & death affair of his future. I felt quite silly in playing *Fête Galante* to him; splendidly as he listened, well as he knows the best bits instantly (of course!) I realised that since he is no longer to be an Opera Director, but a shooting star, the whole thing was unnecessary . . . also my mention of people & things we both loved glided, like the rest, off the marble in spite of a sunny ungenuine smile. I don't mean he wasn't glad to see me . . . but the old Walter has sunk below the horizon. And I thought with pain of Bahr & Anna's diagnosis. I daresay it's a passing phase – & of course I see that sort of thing rather *big* – for I really did love Walter & would still if he'd pull out the vox-humana stop I knew so well. . . .

Wishing you a great time & a safe return in spite of the dangers of the frontier (in Eger it is simply a battlefield . . . shameful) Yours ever ES.

Back at the College in the autumn, the requests of Sir George Henschel were easier to meet.

The Athenaeum, Pall Mall, S.W.1.
Oct.18.1922

My dear Mr. Boult
I wonder if you will think quixotic and impossible what I am going to ask you. But I know you will not mind and there can be no harm in my doing so:
Do you think you could possibly ask Sir Hugh Allen, whom I do not like to bother with a letter, knowing how busy he is from morning till night, whether he would have any objection – provided of course *you* are agreeable – to my running through Liszt's 'Les Préludes' with the College Orchestra at one of your regular practices. I have to conduct that work in Edinburgh – with the Scottish Orchestra – in December and should be most grateful for an opportunity of refreshing my memory. And I thought you might perhaps think it a good practice in sight-reading for those of the orchestra who do not know the work (if there be such). I would not take more than twenty or twenty-five minutes.
But please do not ask Sir Hugh if you think it would be useless. An answer to 7 Cornwall Mansions, Kensington Court, W.8 will much oblige.
We were delighted to have the pleasure of a visit from your sister in Alltnacriche during the Summer and only regretted you had not been with her.
With kind regards believe me
very truly yours
George Henschel.

Of course I would hire the parts and if there is no harp available you might play the part on the piano?

The rehearsal was arranged, and Henschel was delighted.
A year earlier, in November 1921, Adrian Boult had conducted his first concerto with a world-renowned soloist – the Schumann 'Cello Concerto with Pablo Casals. Casals had led off by saying: 'Have we time to work, or must we go straight through it?' It led to a friendship lasting half a century. In the spring, Casals had invited Boult to go out to Barcelona to hear and conduct the Catalan orchestra.

65

I diligently learnt Spanish in order to study his rehearsal methods, but found he always spoke Catalan, a very different proposition . . . I had to be very quick off the mark when I knew that I shouldn't understand what the Maestro said. My musical ear had to do it all.[1]

On his return he wrote an article on Casals and his orchestra for the College Magazine, and this elicited a letter from Casals.

Grosvenor Hotel, London.
12 Dec. 1922

Dear Mr. Boult[2]
    Before leaving England for America I send my good wishes to you and to your mother.
    Your letter has given me great pleasure and the article in 'The R.C.M.' will be a stimulus for me and for my orchestra, for which I owe you gratitude. Apart from the compliments you pay me, your article has the importance of an advertisement for orchestras in general – that is to say, you have shown the necessity for meticulous and conscientious work to benefit and honour orchestral music. A series of articles written by musicians who, like you, make of music a religion would give results I am certain – an orchestra must be an institution of art, of light, of inspiration, and not a machine for concert-making: the day this true point of view is comprehended is the day music will take its true place.
    Madame Casals joins me in sending cordial greetings and congratulations on your success as an artist.
                    Your very devoted
                    Pablo Casals

On 3rd February 1923 Boult was to conduct his first *Dream of Gerontius* with the Royal Choral Society and the Royal Albert Hall Orchestra. He wrote to ask whether Elgar might come to the rehearsal, and raised the question of the higher pitch to which the Albert Hall organ was tuned.

[1] *My own trumpet*, p. 85.   [2] Translated from French.

Brooks's, St. James's Street, S.W.1
Saturday [27th January 1923]

My dear Adrian:
I am leaving on Tuesday morning early & shall be in the country for a few weeks

I detest the high pitch – why could not the *organ* play $\frac{1}{2}$ tone lower? you cannot do *Gerontius* (in that hall especially!) without the O[rgan].

I suppose the O. is tuned to equal temp[eramen]t – but the whole thing is so disastrous that it is quite easy enough to believe it is not tuned at all.

All good wishes
                    Yrs ever
                    Edward Elgar

Another activity of these years was the starting of the Robert Mayer Children's Concerts.

At a later concert we were happy to welcome as guest Mr Walter Damrosch, the distinguished conductor of the New York [Symphony] Orchestra. He had directed children's concerts for many years, and gave us all a delightful object lesson in just how to do it, and how much, or rather how little, to talk.[1]

Hotel de France & Choiseul, 239–241, Rue St. Honoré, Paris.
May 20/1923

My dear Mr. Boult
I remember with so much pleasure your friendliness during my visit to London in January 1922 that I venture to impose on it to the following extent.

I am anxious to see some of the scores of Arnold Bax but do not know who his publishers are.

Could you and would you ask them to send me two or three of his last and latest works to Paris so that I could examine them here as I am afraid I shall not get to London this Summer.

[1] *My own trumpet*, p. 82.

I should also like to get the Ballet music from Holst's comic opera of which I hear charming things.

In fact – any new works by Britishers that seem to you fine, and – if you have the time write me about your doings and Sir Hugh Allen &c. &c.

Please give him my best greetings and if you and he feel that you need a rest from Royal College of Music cares and will fly across the Channel some day next week I'll give you the best dinner Paris can offer.

('I know a bank whereon the wild thyme grows')
Cordially yours
Walter Damrosch

In the spring of 1924 came Boult's election to The Athenaeum, with a congratulatory letter from Elgar:

The Athenaeum, Pall Mall, S.W.1.
Sunday May 4 1924

My dear Adrian: I am so sorry I have been away, – however, the first thing I do on my return is to say 'welcome' to you. – I wish I could have introduced you to this abode of Peace. I fear I am too late for that – but I hope we shall meet here often. I am very proud that I was allowed the honour of proposing you. My love to you,
Yours ever
Edward Elgar

But now the centre of Boult's career was moving away from London. It began with Albert Coates.

Albert Coates was very kind to me and I was often asked to his flat after he came to London in 1919. . . We seem to have forgotten the tremendous impact he made on London music at that time. He gave performances of the classics with a new (to us) warmth and depth of feeling, and his particular battle-horse, the Scriabin *Poem of Ecstasy*, was played again and again to crowded and cheering houses. . . .

I was much touched one day when Albert said he wanted a quiet word with me, just before he was leaving for abroad. So

I went to see him off at Victoria, and he told me that he didn't feel I was getting anywhere in my work, and thought I ought to be doing far more.[1]

Partly as a result of what Coates had said, I decided somewhere about 1922 that though I was having a very happy life in London, I was not really doing a *job* of the kind a conductor ought to have. So I resolved that if nothing developed by the end of 1923 I should go across the Atlantic and see what I could find.

But it was just then that something did develop. Sir Henry Wood resigned the conductorship of the Birmingham Festival Choral Society and nominated Boult as his successor.

Sir Henry told me he only resigned because orchestral conditions were so hopeless: one hectic rehearsal with soloists on the morning of the concert, and no opportunity for the choir to hear the orchestra or get balanced with them, until the concert. He had just tried to do Beethoven's 'Mass' under these conditions, and he couldn't go on. I was in no mood to pick or choose and cheerfully accepted the difficulties. . . . I soon found that I could still concentrate mostly on the choir even at the concert, for a young man named Paul Beard, who in his early twenties had just been promoted to the leadership, could be trusted to lead the orchestra and control it perfectly.

. . . I very soon sensed that the direction of the orchestra might be offered to me. I didn't need to think it over: about fifty concerts in the six winter months with nothing to do in the summer except prepare for the next season, was a plan which suited me perfectly. . . .I shall never forget a very kind letter of welcome which Granville Bantock, Professor of Music at Birmingham, wrote when my appointment was announced.[2]

The University, Edmund Street, Birmingham.
26th March/24

My dear Boult
    I am delighted to hear of our good fortune in the news that you are coming to thrust in your lot with us here by taking

[1] *My own trumpet*, pp. 83–4.   [2] *My own trumpet*, pp. 56–7.

charge of the City Orchestra in addition to the F.Ç.S., & that this means your residence in the Midlands. It has long been my dream to make this city our English Weimar, & the prospects for the realisation of this idea were never brighter than they are today. Your advent will bring new life and culture into the place, & I can promise you the hearty support of the University and School of Music.

I gather that Allen will not want you to give up your work at the R.C.M.; but would you have any time or inclination to help us in any way at the School of Music at the Institute, where we have over 1600 students on the register? Do let me know when you are next in Bham, & let us have a chat on this and other matters concerning future music developments.

Kindest regards & all best wishes
                    Sincerely yours
                    Granville Bantock

At the Midland Institute Boult taught a chamber music class for a short time. But his main energy in Birmingham was directed at improving the orchestral situation. His success in this soon attracted the enthusiastic testimony of Albert Coates.

197, Coleherne Court
S.W.5.
June 4th 1924.

My dear Adrian,
Thank you so much for your nice letter, it is one of the nicest letters I have ever received and you are a dear to have written to me like that.

I am more happy that I can say that you are taking over Birmingham, happy both for you and for Birmingham because you will create something there very much worth while. I am just delighted and I congratulate you most heartily. The few times I conducted there I found them a most appreciative audience so that I feel sure that it is fruitful soil that you are on and that your work will be amply rewarded. I shall take a personal pride in it all and puff myself out with your successes!

70

What especially delights me in the whole thing is the fact that you are going to have daily rehearsals. That is really splendid and you will find it an absolute joy to be with your orchestra day by day.

It is very kind of you to say that you would like me to come down and conduct there at some future time, naturally I shall be delighted to do so and I much appreciate your kind thought of me.

The VERY BEST OF LUCK, my dear Adrian, go ahead with it and don't be discouraged by anything, things may be a bit difficult at first but you'll get there never fear!

With love

Yours as ever

Albert (Coates)

In the autumn of 1925 Holst's new *Choral Symphony* was down for several performances. Boult invited the composer to come and conduct the City of Birmingham Orchestra in October. Replying to this invitation, Holst sent his comments on two articles Boult was writing to analyse the *St. Paul's Suite*.[1]

St. Paul's Girls' School, Brook Green, Hammersmith, W.6. Sep 20 [1925]

Dear Adrian

I agree about having no comma at that place in S P suite. The only other points are

a) In the Ostinato the 2nd violins are usually inaudible to the audience – only the conductor hears them. Just the reverse of our Albert and his six (or is it sixteen) horns in 'no 7 in A' for in that case he is the only man who hears the rest of the orchestra (*if* he hears it!)

Do make a big point in your articles on the difference of the effect from the conductor's stand and from the fourth row of the balcony.

b) In the finale I like two heavy accents in each bar in the 6/8 tune. These are to continue against the 3/4. Kinsey[2] and the

---

[1] *Musical News and Herald*, 7th November 1925, pp. 416, 428.
[2] Herbert Kinsey, principal second violin of the London Symphony Orchestra.

LSO second violins once gave it to me in grand style. The effect was intoxicating.

Unless I hear from you I shall come to rehearsal (G[erald] F[orty] will tell me where) at 10 a.m. on Oct 12 and 13.

Yrs Ever

G

But when it came to the *Choral Symphony* performances, the third movement, *Fancy*, was so complicated to conduct that he asked Boult to direct it, as he wrote to Vally Lasker: '*Fancy* is too much for me so dear Adrian is conducting it tonight . . . Adrian is an Angel with Brains.'

His work at the Royal College of Music expanded to include opera performances, including *Parsifal*.

One of our audiences included Frederic Austin. He asked me to take charge of the *Parsifal* performances of the British National Opera Company, which he then directed, throughout the subsequent winter. It meant a good deal of night travelling, for the company was often in Edinburgh or Newcastle. . . . The company came to Birmingham every winter for two or three weeks, and usually invited me to join them for one performance.[1]

On 1st December 1925 it was *Die Walküre*, and in the audience was Granville Bantock.

26, Wheeley's Road, Edgbaston, Birmingham
Tuesday 1st Dec.
My dear Boult.

I have rarely enjoyed a Wagner Opera so much as the performance of *The Valkyrie* this evening under your beat. You are one of the few men who succeed in bringing one in touch with the master mind which created the music. We were allowed to hear Wagner speaking through the score. Many many thanks – and my profound respects.

Yours ever

Granville Bantock.

It is time the B.N.O.C. invested in a new copy of the Score, or had it rebound.

[1] *My own trumpet*, p. 47.

Soon Bantock wrote again, this time to send his thanks as a composer.

26, Wheeley's Road, Edgbaston, Birmingham.
10 Feb/26

My dear Boult
What can I say to thank you adequately after your superb performance of the *Pagan Chants* last evening? It is a rare, and indeed a real joy to find a colleague with so sympathetic an understanding of one's aims, and these were all realised by you last night. I am more than grateful to you for introducing the *Chants* under such peculiarly favourable conditions & with so great and true an artist as the one & only Frank Mullings. I can only say 'Thank you' again and again, for your generous spirit.
Believe me, my dear Boult,
Gratefully & sincerely yours
Granville Bantock.

At the Royal College of Music, another performance of *Parsifal* evoked a last fond tribute from Frank Schuster.

The Long White Cloud, Bray-on-Thames.
20 July/26

Dearest Adrian
I could not find the right words to express myself last night, and I am not sure that I can now. All I know is that you were the cause of a great joy to me, because you were not only able to revive old memories & particularly – *old thrills* of Bayreuth early days, (the most intense musical emotion of my life) but to add new ones. Also you gave me the gratification of fructifying to the full my belief in you from the very first (and assuredly I *was* the very first as I shall most certainly *not* be the last). I knew you would make a *good* conductor – but it was your interpretation of the last act yesterday that revealed you to me as a *great* one. Illuminated & illuminating, it

brought home to our hearts the inner significance of the subject & the music.

And for this you have the blessing of
Your old friend
Frank S.

The chance to conduct a performance of Mozart's *Cosi fan tutte* at Bristol brought a renewed correspondence with Edward Dent.

10, New Quebec Street, W.1.
17 August 1926

Dear Adrian

Thanks for your letter – I haven't a full score of C.F.T. here, but have found a (wrong) vocal score: however I think I can answer some of your questions.

Act II. sc. vi. *Cessa di molestarmi*,
I don't quite like your *sforzando*, as the 4 soft phrases in the orchestra evidently form a group, and set the emotional feeling – and this makes me feel that when *Fiord*[*iligi*] says '*Cessa di molestarmi*' she doesn't mean it. She is very much in love, and restrained only by propriety. The first part (*aspidi, idra, basilisco*) is all exaggeratedly indignant – it is a parody of operatic emotions: and ends with '*in me solo tu vedi*'. It is quite symmetrical, both in words and music; and absurdly so: then you get another symmetrical & conventional contrast (Adagio – *è vero, è vero*). So I think *Cessa di molestarmi* is not indignation, but (very insincere) 'pleading' – the indignation & return to sense of 'propriety' begins just before *Partiti*

these chords belong to Fiordiligi's phrase, and not to the end of Ferrando's before it – they represent her gesture of drawing herself up stiff, and she must show on the stage that her change of mood makes the orchestra play them. Yes, more or less F: but I think the next pair are louder. She tries to resist, but can't, whenever he looks at her – he says so in the aria.

Yes – I'm sure you're right about the *Sani e salvi* & the pauses – *all* short pauses, I think – just time for a gesture – hat

74

taken off with a sweep, or something of that kind. I should see
it something like this – (about a page back)
(confident & prim in rhythm)
In me fidatevi, ben tutto andrà.
They turn to look at him as he walks towards the door – then
tragic outburst
Mille barbari pensieri – sigh or gasp.
Tormentando il cor mi vanno – look at each other guiltily

ah, di noi che mai sarà? gesture.

ah, di noi che mai sarà? collapse

Ferr[ando] Sani e salvi etc. at top of stage –
Gug[lielmo] fidissime amanti – operatic gesture.

                       walk down & stop on pause.
and so forth – so that they are at the front by the time D.
Alfonso comes in.

    I think the *andante* means Comfortable and *going on*: the
pauses merely mean, give them time if they want to do some
business on the stage. Same for the ladies – it is to allow time
for the 'operatic' manner – wh. your singers will probably
want to indulge in automatically!

    Scene xvi. I think the preceding C major is a quick and fussy
4 in a bar.

    The $E^\flat$ — *Benedetti i doppi conjugi* – is *felt* as 2 in a bar
– though you wd. probably conduct it in 4: rather slower
(crotchets) than the C major – The fuss of the servants is
over, & the guests congratulate politely. You can make a
change of tempo if you like when the 4 soloists sing *Come
par che qui prometta*. a shade slower? picking up a little
at and the Da Capo of the chorus – *Bene-
ditti &c* – might well a little faster
than at first: then you can make a
rallentando on and start a slower sentimen-
tal tempo with the $A^\flat$ part.
This seems to be more definitely 4 in a bar.

75

I always think that with Mozart & all 18th cent music (as Saint-Saëns said) the actual metronome tempo changes very little – he says almost everything ranges between what we shd. now call an Andante and an Allegro moderato. But you get all the contrast you want by style & phrasing – thus in this slow C major opening all rather staccato & detached, the triplets very clearly articulated, and definitely 4 in a bar – just the slightest accents on 2 & 4 to lift it on –

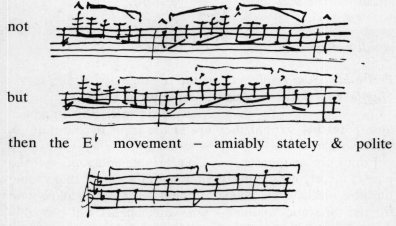

not

but

then the E♭ movement – amiably stately & polite

minims as unit, not crotchets. Even if on the metronome ♩ = ♩ exactly, it will still make a huge difference whether you have crotchets as units (as in C major) or minims (in the E♭). Then in A♭ – 4 smooth crotchets – wh. is very different from the 4 jumpy crotchets of the C major.

Please do anything you like in the secco Recitatives – that's what they're for – & there are great opportunities – wh Strauss used thoroughly to enjoy. But I'm afraid & I have cut most of them down ruthlessly! It is always best if the Conductor can play the secco himself, I think, but is awkward unless you have a special high pianoforte wh. you can play standing. The old harpsichords in Italy were built with long legs – there's a caricature of Pasquini standing at the Keyboard. If you have a small grand pianoforte you can raise it on boxes, and lower the desk so as to be almost flat like a conductor's.

I don't feel strongly on the question of harpsichord or pianoforte for C.F.T. I shd. think that in 1791 Mozart had a pianoforte – It only sounds bad when the conductor makes it sound like Mark Hambourg or a Rolls-Royce grand. You want an elderly Broadwood!

Yours

E. J. Dent

With the Birmingham Choir that season Boult was performing the *Great Service* by William Byrd. This had recently been published by the Oxford University Press, following its rediscovery by the great scholar of Tudor church music, the Rev. E. H. Fellowes. Boult had written to him through Hubert Foss of the Oxford Press.

The Cloisters, Windsor Castle.
Nov. 26th. 1926

My dear Boult

Foss has sent me your letter asking about the Byrd Great Service. I am so glad you are doing it in Birmingham.

Its very existence had been forgotten and when I first saw it in the old MSS in Durham Cathedral I supposed for a moment it was the well known 'short' service known as 'Byrd in D minor'. It quickly became clear that it was a much larger & more important work. Then I transcribed & scored it and found that two voice parts were missing from the Durham books. Of these one (a bass part) turned up later in another set of the Durham MSS – an extremely lucky chance, for there was no duplicate of any of the other voice parts in this other set. Then a little more text turned up in Peterhouse, a duplicate of one of the tenor parts at Worcester, & some fragments in the BM in the hand of John Baldwin. Peterhouse supplied the missing alto part of the Evening Canticles & the Baldwin some fragments of the missing alto in the Te Deum. The rest of the missing text was supplied by myself to the best of my ability.

The work was printed complete in Vol II of Tudor Ch[urch]

77

Music, which was entirely edited by me; & subsequently a transposed acting edition followed from which no doubt you are singing on the present occasion.

The enclosed cuttings may perhaps give you information. I should like them back some time or other –

I hope you are flourishing

Yours sincerely

Edmund H. Fellowes.

Boult then asked about matters of interpretation.

The Cloisters, Windsor Castle.
Dec. 15th. 1926

My dear Boult

It is perfectly splendid that you and your chorus should be working so enthusiastically at the Byrd Great Service. I would certainly have come to hear it on Jan. 23rd. but we are sailing for Canada two days before that.

As to tempi; do whatever seems good to you. I think the whole spirit of interpretation of Tudor music is based upon freedom. And one can put it as baldly as that to people like yourself who would not misunderstand my meaning. It is all-important to make sure that it is vital. If at any point it seems to flag in interest one may go faster or slower. It is always possible that the actual music may flag in interest at one point or another, but such occurrences are rare in Byrd. You express it admirably when you speak of 'giving the amazing expressiveness of the work full play.' Do that, and you can't go wrong.

All good wishes

Yours sincerely

E. H. Fellowes.

In March 1927, at the Holst Festival in Cheltenham, Boult again came to the composer's rescue as conductor. Holst's daughter Imogen describes the occasion:

He was not very strong at the time, and it was doubtful whether he would be able to conduct the whole of *The Planets*

78

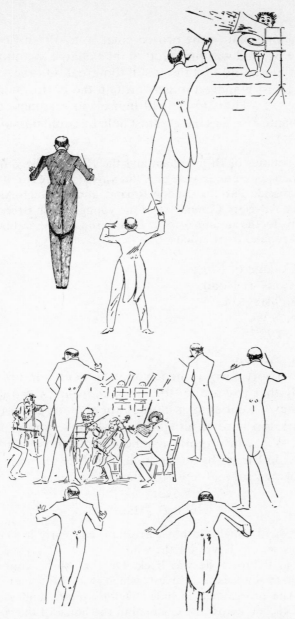

A school concert with the Birmingham City Orchestra at Rugby,
ca. 1926: anonymous impressions on the back of a programme.

in the second half of the programme. But Adrian Boult was standing by, and was prepared to take charge at a moment's notice if he should find the strain too great. On the strength of this, Holst managed to get through the performance successfully. . . . That Boult held himself in readiness to conduct if wanted . . . was the greatest help he could possibly have had.[1]

To the duties of Birmingham and the Royal College of Music were added appointments as Percy Pitt's assistant at Covent Garden and – alongside Pitt, Sir Landon Roland, and Sir Hugh Allen – to the Music Advisory Committee of the young British Broadcasting Company. By the autumn of 1927 Boult's run-down condition drew a typical rebuke from Allen.

Royal College of Music,
Prince Consort Road,
South Kensington,
London, S.W.7.
Oct. 21. 1927

My dear Adrian

I am so very sorry to hear you have been laid up. I hope sincerely that you are on the mend thoroughly & rapidly.

You never wear enough clothes nor do you eat enough – & you work too hard & altogether misbehave yourself pretty royally. Will you promise amendment in those respects & rejoice your friends by taking some little care of yourself if not for your own sake at least for theirs

Yours ever
Hugh P. Allen

The persistent cough did not leave him, and early in December Boult was sent to Egypt for the winter.

Early in February he was back. On the 9th he conducted a Birmingham Orchestra concert which was broadcast by the B.B.C. The programme included Delius's *Paris*, and the transmission reached across the Channel to the home of the composer himself.

[1] *Gustav Holst* (Oxford University Press, 1938), pp. 122–3.

Grez-sur-Loing
10.2.28

My dear Boult,

Your performance of 'Paris' last night, which I heard through the Radio, gave me the greatest pleasure. I felt you were in entire sympathy with the work and your tempi were all just as I want them.

Now and again the Wireless faded (Daventry Experimental unfortunately always does that), but I got an excellent impression.

With kind remembrances from my wife and with many thanks

Yrs sincerely
Frederick Delius

When the composer was closer at hand, things did not always go so smoothly. A revival of Ethel Smyth's *The Wreckers* in honour of the composer's 70th birthday resulted in a fearful fracas – when it suddenly seemed to that formidable lady that her masterpiece was being muddled. Boult wrote a calming letter.

Coign Woking.
29th March 1928

My *dear* Mr. Boult   Your letter made me so happy – As long as people are fond of each other nothing else matters & what made me so *miserable* was feeling that you seemed to have got me all wrong & to hate me. You see, at tennis, when I was 16, I remember a niece of the Empress Eugénie's whom I loved saying to me 'You beat me at tennis because you look so fierce, as if you were going to *swallow the ball*, that I can't hit it back properly!!' I have a Gutta-percha countenance & have terrific energy, of course, & that makes me *look* as if I were fearfully excited or fearfully angry or something when, if my face were less dramatic, anyone would see it amounts to next to nothing really! And I would be as incapable of savaging an 'inferior', as we think of them (like Shephard[1]) as of thrashing a dog cruelly! Moreover I knew all the time that it *wasn't his*

[1] Manager and librarian of the Birmingham City Orchestra.

81

fault & really only wanted particulars so as to try & get on the trail of the only *mainly* correct set (as far as I know). This absence of malice or unfairness anyone (if given time) would feel in one second however agitated & frantic I might look (I'm thinking of Shephard) – & orchestras & choruses always feel it –

Dear Mr. Boult . . . once you say that to yourself – once you realise how the thought of your (apparently) hating me gave me real sharp pain, I *know* I shan't get on your nerves – (if I see I do, I shall say 'Basingstoke'!) It was only because you were frantic (of course) at the *Wreckers* incident . . . & so was I (equally of course) – and *not* because you & I can't be trusted to wield the stick on the same evening without beating each other – that bourasques occurred! *On the contrary* I long to take part in a show *with you* as soon as possible! I do admire you & your work so – and I know what you are *in your heart*. And I believe you know (*really* down below) what I am in mine. And that, my dear friend, is all that really matters –

I'm off to Berlin tomorrow after a horrible incident at Bristol which makes me almost despair of human nature. But I had a jolly rehearsal (choral) & arrived home pretty cooked.

After this Jubilee Year no more choral rehearsing etc for me! Bless you – & DON'T LET yourself get 'bad tempered' (which you *say* you are becoming??) There's a sort of moral Bicarb. of Soda of which a pinch taken daily really does correct one's acidity – if only one remembers to take it. . . . Anyhow as regards you & me I now feel *safe for all time* . . . & that means so much to

> Yours always
> Ethel Smyth

Through summer holidays, he extended to Oxford his teaching of an art in which he was now recognised as a leading master. The following item appeared on 9th August 1928 in *The Daily Telegraph*:

By precept and example Dr. Adrian Boult, musical director of the Birmingham City Orchestra, yesterday, sought to impart some of the secrets of the 'difficult art' of wielding the

82

conductor's baton to students attending, at Oxford, the Summer Course in Music Teaching.

Under his direction nearly 300 men and women wielded batons for the first time in their lives.

Dr. Boult described the various movements connected with conducting as an engineering principle. 'In most cases,' he said, 'the first two fingers and the thumb are the only parts needed to bring the baton into effective play. For bigger things the wrist, then the elbow, and lastly, the shoulder, may be brought into action, but only on very rare occasions, such as when you may be called upon to conduct a Handel festival, will you be called upon to use your whole arm.'

Control of the baton was one of the most difficult things to acquire. 'It is impossible to pick it up in a day,' remarked Dr. Boult. 'You will shed as many tears and go through as many labours as will a violinist before he obtains perfect mastery of his instrument.

'It is not at all necessary to do this sort of thing,' he said, striking an imposing attitude and bending his little finger in mid-air in a graceful curve. 'It only attracts the attention of everyone to the finger instead of the baton. It must be practice, practice, practice. Keep a stick everywhere. I always have one lying on my desk and I pick it up at all sorts of odd moments and fool about with it, so that the handling of it becomes almost second nature. Even when people come in to talk I invariably twiddle the thing about in my hand. It is quite good to do this and practise with it on the desk, and also on a friend, too, sometimes. (Laughter.)

'Be careful that your baton does not slip,' said Dr. Boult. A second later the baton with which he was demonstrating slipped through his fingers and fell to the floor, much to the amusement of the students.

Then Boult took over direction of the London Bach Choir from Vaughan Williams.

Glorydene Dorking
Oct 14 [1928]

Dear Adrian

Thank you so much for your letter.

I know the choir will make great strides with you. I have already heard an enthusiastic account of the first practice.

I enclose a (confidential) list of singers who would do for semi-chorus.

I used to find Lady Gowers a splendid help in arranging the choir-seating for performances, discovering semi-chorus singers etc.

I feel rather diffident about offering advice to such an experienced chorus trainer as you but I will chance my arm & make the following suggestions –

(1) Don't wait to start practice till everybody is ready – or you will never start at all. I always used to kick off at 5-30 sharp whoever was or wasn't there & however much row was going off at the bargain counter behind the curtain.

(2) Always insist on 2 band rehearsals – The extra rehearsal only costs about £25 which is a drop in the ocean compared with our total loss on each concert. I used to have full rehearsal 4 to 7 the day before the concert, telling the chorus to come at 4-30 or 5 as the case might be – They were very good about it & I got most of the females there by 4-30 & usually had the full chorus there from 5-30 to 6-45 when the band used to disappear & I sometimes kept the chorus on alone up to 7 or later.

Then I had a band rehearsal with soloists & such of the chorus as could turn up at 10 am on the day of the concert.

Yrs
RVW

Early in 1929 there was promise of an appearance in New York to repeat a Birmingham concert in which Myra Hess and Harold Samuel had played three double concertos by Bach and Mozart. Then it transpired that the New York orchestra, the Barrère Ensemble, did not appear without its conductor-founder Georges Barrère. Myra Hess's howl of disappointment came across the Atlantic.

84

The Saint Hubert, 120 West 57th Street, New York.
January 29th 1929

My dear Adrian

As a matter of fact it is January 30th – as it is 1 A.M.! but if I don't send you a line now, I shall despair of ever having an undisturbed moment.

I can't tell you what a disappointment it is to Harold & me that you will not be conducting for us on Feb. 5th. Our faces fell, & we really felt quite desperate when we arrived & were told of the terrible difficulties here in getting a few players together.

I had to rush away from here the day after our arrival & while I was spending endless days, & nights, to the Middle West & back – everything was finally arranged. I was so upset, when I got back, to hear that there had been some misunderstandings about the cables which were sent to you, or Ibbs & Tillett? Anyhow, it is quite 'damnable' – & we shall miss you terribly.

Is this a glorious career????

Today, I happen to have had an enjoyable recital with Jelly – but the concerts one *really* looks forward to are few and far between!

I have also heard Gabrilowitsch conduct the Brahms 2nd Symphony – & a 'piece' called *The Haunted Castle* by Josef Hofmann!!!! (It sounded like a birthday party given by Liszt to Wagner!!)

We have also had a little party here – so it has been a typical New York day! Hence this scribble – but I could not let another day go without sending you a line –

You really can't imagine how disappointed we are – If you ever feel like writing – 'letters from home' are a tremendous solace when one is travelling week after week in this wonderful, but bewildering country!

With my love and curses!

Myra

II. British Broadcasting
1929–1950

Somewhere near my fortieth birthday in the spring of 1929 I had an urgent letter from Walford Davies. He and Sir John (later Lord) Reith and Sir Hugh Allen had been having some earnest conversations. Percy Pitt's time as Director of Music of the B.B.C. was to come to an end, under the age rule, on 1 January 1930, and they all felt I might succeed him. Would I go and stay a night with him at Windsor and talk it over?

As before with the Birmingham decision, there was no doubt about what was right, though I felt it might well be far less pleasant. In fact, it was made quite clear to me at my first talk with Sir John Reith that I was to *direct* the music. If conducting now and then could be added to direction without impairing it, well and good, but the direction was the principal thing, and Sir John added that he did not like sending for his Director of Music in the afternoon only to be told that he had gone home to rest as he was conducting that evening.[1]

Six months of negotiation led to this letter from the B.B.C.'s Director General:

Savoy Hill,
London, W.C.2.
26th November, 1929.

Dear Mr. Boult,
Further to our conversation to-day, and to your letter of November 22nd, as you know there is no divergence of opinion between us on any matter contained in the latter.

With regard to outside policy, there is no comment on points 1, 2 and 3. With respect to 4, I remarked that the

[1] *My own trumpet*, p. 94.

86

Corporation's support of local organisations is desirable and should be prosecuted as in the past, consistent, however, with the fact that our actual responsibility is to listeners, and that there can be no claim for local support as a matter of right. This you quite agreed with.

As to procedure, you will be what is, or should be, implied in the term 'Music Director'; that is, a responsible departmental chief under the Head of the Programme Branch, with authority to deal as you wish with all the staff of that Department, and with the work thereof (comprehending not only Headquarters but all Provincial Stations) in the administrative and artistic sense, subject to consultation on what might be termed matters of policy importance with Mr. Eckersley, and when necessary with me or the Board. As you know, Mr. Eckersley has no objection to your coming to see me at any time. As to whether or not the weekly meeting of the Music Department is continued is a matter for you to settle, and you will of course attend any meetings of the Programme Branch.

I think I have covered above your points 1–4, with the exception of the Music Advisory Committee. In this connection, it is certainly the intention of the Corporation that you should attend their meetings regularly.

With respect to paragraph 5, there are, as you know, office hours and office procedure, but senior and responsible officials realise what is incumbent upon them and are not tied down to a routine. There should be no difficulty between you and Mr. Eckersley on this point.

No. 6 is agreed.

Respecting the date of appointment:-

1. I attach a draft announcement; Wd you like it amplified? I think it might contain a summary of your career – will you do this?

2. You will write this, and perhaps you will send it to me not later than the middle of April;

3. I understand you will take up your appointment definitely on May 15th, but to such extent as is possible between the beginning of the year and then, you will come here, particularly in order to deal with any policy matters which have to be

settled during that period, and generally to take up any special points you may wish to investigate. You will not be considered responsible for the Music Department, but on the other hand, it will be arranged with Mr. Eckersley that 'what you say goes'.

I think this settles the whole matter, and I should like to say once again how much we are looking forward to your association with us in a position which, in our judgment, and according to Sir Hugh Allen's statement, is at least second to none in musical importance in the country.

Yours sincerely,

J. C. W. Reith

But Boult's appointment to the B.B.C. had been a matter of public knowledge for months. Many friends had written at the first moment: one was Granville Bantock.

Metchley Lodge, Harborne, Birmingham.
1st May 1929

My dear Boult

I was delighted to see the confirmation of your appointment to the B.B.C. in tonight's *Evening Dispatch*. This is indeed good news for all lovers of good music, and everyone is to be congratulated, including the Public & the B.B.C. There are sure to be difficult times ahead, but you will have the loyal support of all true musicians. Long may you reign.

Best and heartiest wishes from

Yours ever

Granville Bantock.

An older friend, going back to Oxford days, was Frank Howes. He was to summarise Boult's career for *The Radio Times*, dwelling particularly on the experience of the Royal College of Music:

At the R.C.M. he was confronted by experimental scores to be tried out at Patron's Fund Rehearsals, and it was Sir Hugh Allen's opinion that Boult is the safest conductor to whom a new work can be entrusted at short notice. His catholicity and versatility is such that he will make a good job of any score entrusted to him. The importance of this quality in his new post is apparent. He may not have to conduct all and sundry kinds of music, but he will have to adjust competing claims for space in the B.B.C. programmes.[1]

This point also struck a writer for *Musical Opinion*:

. . . There will be just a little piquancy in the notion of Mr. Boult, a contemner hitherto of much orchestral music the public has taken to its heart, deciding on the relative merits of 'I kiss your hand, Madame' or 'I faw down and go BOOM' as constituents of a dance music programme.[2]

Within a year Boult was to have his own repertoire of after-dinner stories on this subject. *The Star* reported:

Dr. Adrian Boult, musical director of the B.B.C., whose classical concerts are so much admired, was also a guest of honour at the dinner. He told a delightful story, as recounted by one of the 'uncles' of the B.B.C., who said that one of his little nieces included in her prayers one evening the request: 'Please, Jesus, make Mr. Boult ill for Christmas, so that we may have some jolly music.'[3]

In fact the programme-planning was the most demanding aspect of directing the B.B.C.'s music, as Boult himself explained in a series of lectures at the Royal Institution. These were printed in the B.B.C. magazine *The Listener*.

. . . The whole body of programmes must be so chosen and arranged as to implement the general programme policy of the B.B.C.; in other words the gigantic crossword-puzzle must not merely be solved – it must have a definite meaning when it is finished. There must also be correlation between the programme activities and experience in London and the B.B.C.'s parallel activities throughout the country, again with an eye to the varied problems of programme balance. The scheme for the week thus sketched is then handed to the different departments, and we musicians must consider how we can artistically fill the spaces, allocate the various groups of the orchestra and other resources into these periods, and

[1] *The Radio Times*, 27th June 1930.   [2] *Musical Opinion*, July 1929.
[3] 4th February 1931.

set about the engagement of artists and building of pro-grammes.

. . . There are then various departmental experts to be considered; organ music, for instance, is in the hands of one member of the Music Department; chamber music of another; contemporary music, if there is to be a modern programme in the week, is naturally in the hands of an expert; and then there is the group whose function it is to deal with the artists we engage . . .

Every year we have a series, once a month through the winter, of what we call Contemporary Concerts, partly chamber and partly orchestral. Here outstanding novelties from Europe are performed, sometimes by their composers, or by friends of the composers who may be considered to have specialised in these performances, and here too there are two or three programmes devoted to the most modern expression of English music. . . . Taking the B.B.C. music staff as a whole, we are all of us in one way or another in personal contact with the composers in this country who count. It is not likely that any of them would be planning an important new work without one of us knowing about it.

Now, what about the younger men, the unknown compos-ers who are trying to write? Are we helping them adequately? A great many people think we are not, and perhaps therefore you will allow me to tell you what we do. Every February an enormous pile of new manuscript scores accumulates at the B.B.C., and three or four of our most sensitive and critical musicians are relieved of a good deal of their work in order that they may spend their time going through these new scores. The harvest is not great – in fact it is distressingly small – and I know that some of my composer friends consider that the B.B.C. is very much to blame for this. I wonder if we are?

It is always hard to draw a line in cases of this kind, and it would not be difficult for me to tell our judges to draw their line somewhat lower and accept more work. As it is, a certain number of border-line works or works whose scoring does not readily give the judge an opportunity of hearing how it would come off, are put down for some special rehearsals which are

90

devoted to new works, under the guidance of a competent conductor, usually in the presence of the composer, and the decision taken after hearing them; and I must, I am afraid, emphasise what is at a moment's thought obvious to everybody, that the B.B.C. exists primarily for the benefit of its listeners and not for the benefit of young composers, any more than for young performers and conductors. . . . I myself am not particularly interested in first performances as such. I feel it is more important to give second and third performances of important new works rather than to let it have a first performance and then be allowed to drop, as has often occurred in the past.[1]

Boult made it clear from the outset that he would not give up his conducting. By mid-1930 he was in full stride in two positions – as Director of Music with an office in Savoy Hill and a devoted secretary, Mrs. Gwen Beckett (who is with him still nearly half a century later); and as conductor of the new B.B.C. Symphony Orchestra. It was as a practical and experienced musician that his advice was sought by Gustav Holst over a technical problem in the composer's new *Choral Fantasia*, op. 51.

St. Paul's Girls' School, Brook Green, Hammersmith, W.6.
Oct 3 [1930]

Dear Adrian
  You are too busy a man to be bothered unless the matter is urgent. The matter in point is my bewilderment as to how to bar my new thing now it is fully sketched.[2] I want to collect conductors' opinions and am going to HJW[ood] on Sunday. It isn't exactly urgent because I ought to decide it for myself. But I'd feel much happier if I could talk it over with you. I fear

[1] *The Listener*, 21st December 1932, pp. 880–1.
[2] Imogen Holst writes: '. . . The passage where he was bewildered by the bar-lines occurs at the words "Then he hideth his face" [the six bars before figure VIII]. It was eventually printed with the time signature 8/4, but I have recently come across a scribbled entry in his notebook for October 1930, saying: 'Ch/Fan 8/4 dotted lines – Prefer 3/4 3/4 2/4 for voices – Don't be logical Decide each case by other parts" '. ('Holst's music: some questions of style and performance at the centenary of his birth', in *Proceedings of the Royal Music Association*, 1974, pp. 205–6.)

it would mean nearly or quite an hour. And I'd be quite miserable if you gave up that hour when you didn't oughter – when, for instance, you ought to be walking about a garden in Hampshire!

Would you kindly pass on enclosed application for tickets?

Good-Luck to the concert

Yr Ever

G

Are you continuing the Monday chamber concerts of modern music? If so, may I come?

After a short winter holiday, Boult wrote about broadcasting a week of Holst's music. The programmes included the short chamber opera *Savitri* and *The Planets*.

British Broadcasting Corporation
Savoy Hill, London W.C.2
13th January, 1931.

Dear Gustav,

We are doing *Savitri* soon, I believe, at a studio performance, and I was wondering whether you would like to have fuller Strings at any time or whether we shall stick to the double quartet.

I have discovered that in my score of Mercury on page 55, the bar before figure IV, the E flat entry of the First Horn has been changed to E natural. Is this right, please?

Yours ever,

Adrian

St. Paul's Girls' School,
Brook Green, Hammersmith, W.6.
Jan 18 [1931]

Dear Adrian

Welcome home! I hope Sicily meant as much to you as it did to me.

The horn note in Mercury should be E♮ not ♭ and the fault was the composer's who was a bigger ass than usual when he let the ♭ slip in.

Will you decide about the strings in *Savitri*. I don't know what is best for broadcasting but I am all in favour of leaving the score as it is because I've usually found that solo instruments come through so well.

Thank you very much for doing it. May I come and bring 3 or 4 friends?

I've heard a rumour that the BBC tried to get Dorothy Silk to sing *Savitri* on Feb 13 but found that she was engaged. If it is not a) too late b) too interfering would you consider altering the date? DS does it so beautifully.

But *don't* consider it if you've approached anyone else.

I wish we could meet more in 1931. Barring Mondays a 1.30 lunch is nearly always as possible as it would be jolly for me. If the same ever applies to you let me know. But you speak first as you're the busier. And I suggest 'no treating'.

Yr coming performance of *Savitri* has awakened my old dream of writing a real radio opera. But it remains a dream.

> Y Ever
> Gustav

Further broadcast plans included the Suite *Beni Mora* and two Motets op. 43 to be performed by the B.B.C. Wireless Singers under the direction of their conductor Stanford Robinson.

St. Paul's Girls' School,
Brook Green, Hammersmith, W.6.
Feb 6 [1931]

Dear Adrian

I'm sending the motets to you separately. *Don't bother to acknowledge them*. I'm also sending them to St Robinson.

Re telephoning, please do so as often as possible (especially if there's a chance of a meal together) but whenever an immediate answer is not wanted, tell the porter to leave a message for me in his room.

I'm going to be a further bother about tickets. And I think the best way is to write to Mrs Beckett and bother her – to make my motto for 1931 'Bother Mrs Beckett'.

But in order to make it quite respectable and to insure that

I'm not asking too much I'm enclosing the letter in this for you to censure if necessary.

I'm doubtful whether I can come on the 15th so *please* rehearse *Beni Mora* EARLY on the morning of the 14th – I'm going to Cambridge for the *Fairy Queen* in the afternoon.

What a wonderful week you are giving me! Bless you

Gustav

After the week of Holst's music in February 1931, Boult wrote about the possibility of an orchestral version of his Prelude and Scherzo *Hammersmith*, recently completed as a commission for the B.B.C. Military Band to play under their director B. Walton O'Donnell. Among the composer's friends *Hammersmith* had come to be known familiarly as 'Emma'.

British Broadcasting Corporation
Savoy Hill, London, W.C.2
11th March, 1931.

Dear Gustav,

First of all I have got to say how sorry I am that I have made a terrible mistake and agreed to the postponement of the day on which I am to talk about you over the wireless to March 27th, completely ignoring the fact that I have to do a Studio Orchestral Concert at the same moment. I cannot think how I can have been so idiotic, but there it is, and I am going to ask Victor-Hely-Hutchinson to do the Talk for me, if you don't mind. We will go through things together beforehand, and I think there will be gramophone illustrations, which I have no doubt he will be able to play as well as I can – there is every possibility of his doing the Talk considerably better.

You know that it is necessary that we should keep our eyes open for new work here, as well as old things. If 'Emma' would be suitable or there is any chance of your giving us some other new work as well I need hardly say how delighted we should be, and personally how delighted I should be if I were allowed to take charge of it.

Yours ever
Adrian

St. Paul's Girls' School,
Brook Green, Hammersmith, W.6.
March 13 [1931]

Dear Adrian

Bless you but you forgot the One Important Matter – how are you?

Get Mrs Beckett to send me her private opinion on this point. I'm hoping to have a week's middle-aged walking in Normandy from the 27th so shall miss the talk.

I shall send Emma to you first. I'd rather you and the BBC orchestra introduced her than anyone else.

If you'd like my two pianists [Vally Lasker and Nora Day] to come and play her to you as they did to O'Donnell they'd be proudanappy to do so. Or would you like to hear the military version?[1]

No need to reply.

Y Ever

G

At the same time Boult had sent a similar request for new music to Holst's great friend Ralph Vaughan Williams. He particularly asked about *Job*.

The White Gates, Westcott Road, Dorking.
[undated, received at B.B.C. 23rd March 1931]

Dear Adrian

I owe you 2 answers

(1) To your letter of March 10
I have ½ finished a p[iano]f[or]te concerto which Harriet Cohen is to play if she likes it – But (a) it may never be finished (b) I may not like when it is (c) she may not – so that's that. Please say nothing about it at present.

(2) *Job* – with great pleasure – a pfte arrt. is being done now & will be ready soon – Of course I shd. be proud if you wd conduct it – (the score is legible)

Yrs

R Vaughan Williams

[1] The military band version was to be given an informal trial in B.B.C. Studio 10 on 23rd April 1931.

Boult pursued the question of the Vaughan Williams Piano Concerto.

The White Gates, Westcott Road, Dorking.
April 5 1931

Dear Adrian

Many thanks for your letter – Probably the inchoate Concerto had better stand over and *please say nothing about it to anyone* as it may all come to nothing –

You ask about neglected masterpieces by me. About 20 years ago I had a piece played called *In the Fen Country* which I rather liked then – I will look it out one day and see whether I still like it enough to submit it for your disapproval

Yrs
RVW

Now another voice sounded which had been silent for years – that of Elgar. At the Hereford Festival of 1924 Adrian Boult had told Elgar of his plan to produce *The Dream of Gerontius* at Birmingham with a reduced body of woodwind on account of expense. The old composer was stung to the quick – he said because of his long associations with Birmingham, where *Gerontius* had been first produced in 1900. But his own loneliness since his wife's death might well have sharpened his distress that the young man on whom he set such high hopes could support such an abridgement – even as a practical measure for getting the work performed again at a time when Elgar's music was falling out of favour. In the event, Boult himself had paid for the extra wind players and given the full performance in Birmingham in October 1924, but he had been on distant terms with Elgar ever since. Now he felt the impossibility of this position as the B.B.C.'s Director of Music – especially with Elgar's 75th birthday on the horizon in June 1932. He asked their mutual friend W. H. Reed (leader of the London Symphony Orchestra) to try to put things right between them. Elgar responded instantly.

Marl Bank, Rainbow Hill, Worcester.
12th April 1931

My dear Adrian: I need not tell you that I am delighted to be allowed to address you in the old way: I learned from dear

96

Billy Reed that you wd. like things to be as they were long ago: I will refer to the ancient matter for one moment now & never again. My feelings were acute: I have never had a real success in life – commercially never: so all I had (& have now) was the feeling* that I had written *one* score which satisfied R. Strauss, Richter & many others; it was the discovery that no one in that very wealthy city – which always pretended to be proud of the production of Gerontius – cared a straw whether the work was presented as I wrote it or not: *there* at least I hoped to be recognised. Now let us forget it.

Reed tells me interesting things about a suggested notice of my 75th birthday: naturally I feel grateful & interested & shall be glad to work, or sympathise only, with you in this & in any artistic work you are engaged upon.

Best regards with all sincere good wishes

I am

Your old friend

Edward Elgar

P.S. Forgive a hurried & untidy note: I would not wait to make a manufactured epistle – you will understand

* I will not trouble to put the tenses right here

Newbury
15 April 1931

My dear Sir Edward,

I can't tell you what a thrill it was to see your writing again on an envelope addressed to me. Your letter only caught me up here this morning & I must write to thank you for it with all my heart. Willie told me it was coming, & this was an added pleasure. He will have told you *my* feelings about it all, so there is nothing more to say about it, now that the expression of want of confidence which hurt me so much (coming as it did after such enormous kindness from you), is effectively & permanently washed out by your offer to help us over your Birthday Festival next year.

Will you think over what form you would like it to take? The present position is that nothing has been done (re financial sanction &c) with the B.B.C. authorities, but a few of our music people have just talked it over. Our present idea is to suggest about 4 concerts (Chorus & orchestra), but whether we should aim for superb performances of the better-known works or at bringing forward less-known ones, or both, or in what proportion, is what I should much like to consult you about.

As it happens, I am going to a meeting in Birmingham late on Saturday night (driving from Bristol) & returning to Salisbury early on Sunday. It will be a tight fit, as regards time, in both directions, but if I can run in to see you even for 10 minutes, I should love to do so. I shall be at Torquay (c/o Festival) on Thursday & Friday, but do not trouble to write please, I will telephone to see if you are in & can see me, as I come past. I think you must be near the main road.

May I just repeat what a joy it was to get your letter & to look forward to seeing you again, very soon I hope. It will be splendid to feel that the glorious work of performing your music is again quite free of any personal regret.

With *my* many thanks

Yours always Adrian.

P.S. For your guidance in planning it may be of interest just to note what has been done or is already planned apart from the Festival, though none of this need be *excluded* – it will in fact be good to include some as they will already be known.

18 Feb 1931 E ♭ Symphony (ACB)
25 Feb 1931 Violin Concerto (Sammons, ACB)
6 May 1931   Variations (ACB)
18 May 1931 *Gerontius* (National Chorus – Stanford Robinson)
Winter 1931–2 (possibly in November) [Landon] Ronald's concert will probably be an Elgar programme – he has suggested *Falstaff* & the *Sea Pictures*. Also the first Symphony is on the first draft, either for Wood or A.C.B.

The meeting was a happy one, and a series of three Elgar concerts were arranged for 1932 – two of them with the direct participation of Elgar himself.

Gustav Holst was preparing his *Choral Fantasia* for its first performance at Gloucester. He sent this post card on Boult's leaving for a short summer holiday abroad and in reply to a suggestion for luncheon on 16th July.

St. Paul's Girls' School, Brook Green, Hammersmith, W.6.
June 11 [1931]

Bon Voyage and A Riverderci, On July 16 I rehearse at Gloucester and am walking there from Oxford so if we lunch on the 14th it would have to be at Bibury. I'm seeing Mrs Jones on Monday and will see about going to Gregynog. Friday is nearly always a good day for me. You know, of course, that the middle period alchemists always gave Spider (male) as a preventive from seasickness.[1]

Yr Ever G

Boult's own broadcasts often brought responses in distinguished quarters. A broadcast performance of *Die Walküre* from Covent Garden elicited a typically lavish panegyric from Bernard Shaw.

Ayot St. Lawrence, Welwyn, Herts.
13th. Oct. 1931

Dear Adrian Boult
Blessings on you! I have at last heard 'Nicht weis'ich dir mehr Helden zur Wahl' properly conducted, and consequently properly sung, after hearing one wretched Wotan after another whacked through it as if he were the Count di Luna trumpeting 'Per me ora fatale'. And at Covent Garden too! What is the world coming to?
Also 'Der Augen leuchtendes Paar' taken at the right time.
And the band not a mob but a concert.
Don't trouble to acknowledge this. I thought I'd send it because people who know the difference ought occasionally to say so as a sort of tuning note.

faithfully, G. Bernard Shaw

More Holst performances were coming on, including the first performance of *Hammersmith* in its orchestral version (scheduled

[1] Imogen Holst writes: 'The reference is to Carl van Vechten's book about Hollywood, called *Spider Boy*, which my father was very fond of.

99

for a Queen's Hall broadcast concert under Boult on 25th November) and *The Perfect Fool*.

St. Paul's Girls' School,
Brook Green, Hammersmith, W.6.
Oct. 19th, 1931.

Dear Adrian,

Thanks for card. I hope to come to Studio 10 on November 16th at 9, but regret that the rehearsal is impossible. I presume it is the Ballet and not the complete opera. May I bring about a dozen people?

I hope to send *Hammersmith* on November 2nd, score and parts complete. Will you tell the programme writer that so far as the work owes anything to outside influences it is the result of living in Hammersmith for thirty nine years on and off and wanting to express my feelings for the place in music; also it is the result of a B.B.C. invitation to write something for their military band; and, just as I was going to start on the work I read A. P. Herbert's *Water Gipsies*. There is no programme and no attempt to depict any person or incident. The only two things that I think were in my mind were 1) a district crowded with cockneys, which would have been overcrowded if it was not for the everlasting good humour of the people concerned and 2) the background of the river, that was there before the crowd and will be there presumably long after, and which goes on its way largely unnoticed and apparently quite unconcerned. Let me know rehearsal times as soon as you can.

Yours ever,
Gustav

St. Paul's Girls' School,
Brook Green, Hammersmith, W.6.
Nov. 2nd, 1931.

Dear Adrian,

I had hoped to have sent Emma to you, but owing to a mistake in some of the parts I fear I cannot send it before tomorrow evening or Wednesday morning. I hope the delay will not bother you. I have been told to send the parcel to the Musical Librarian,

B.B.C. I have promised to send one of the piano duet copies for use in the control [room monitoring the broadcast]. The copy will be in the wrong key and there are various differences, including bars added or omitted, as the piano version agrees with the military band score. I will send the piano part on Friday afternoon. I hope to come to all the rehearsals.

With regard to pace, the Prelude should flow calmly and fairly slowly, without being impressive, and the Scherzo should be as quick as possible, as long as it sounds easy and good-tempered and not brilliant, hard or efficient. In short, it must sound like London and not Paris.

Yours ever,
Gustav

Hammersmith was broadcast from Queen's Hall on 25th November.

A performance of *Brigg Fair* by Delius on 21st February 1932 brought a note of appreciation from the old and infirm composer.

Grez-sur-Loing, Seine-et-Marne.
Feb.22.1932

Dear Boult,

I listened in last night, and want to tell you that I have never heard a better performance of *Brigg Fair*. Everything came through wonderfully distinctly, and you gave me a great deal of pleasure for which I thank you most heartily.

Sincerely yours,
Frederick F. Delius

In return, Boult was able to give further news of a big project to broadcast Delius's opera *A Village Romeo and Juliet* with Sir Thomas Beecham.

The British Broadcasting Corporation,
Savoy Hill, London, W.C.2
29th February 1932.

Dear Mr. Delius,

Very many thanks for troubling to write about the performance of *Brigg Fair*. I am so delighted to hear you thought it was a good one. We all worked very hard as we thought you might be listening.

We are so much looking forward to the performance of *Romeo and Juliet*. Beecham prepared everything before he went off to America, and I hope he will come back to find everything in good order.

Yours sincerely,
Adrian C. Boult.

And then, amid preparations for the Elgar 75th birthday festival, came a proposal of a different sort.

The British Broadcasting Corporation,
Savoy Hill, London, W.C.2
22nd February, 1932.

Dear Sir Edward

We are on the point of completing a contract with H.M.V. for the recording of the B.B.C. Orchestra. They want chiefly familiar things to start with, and one of the works they want to get done very soon is Chopin's Funeral March. I do not remember the standard orchestration of it very well, but it occurred to us that if you would be interested to reorchestrate it, it would be a wonderful thing for us. If you feel like bothering yourself in this way I shall be very happy to communicate with H.M.V. and ask them to take up the business side of it with you direct, but I thought I would just ask you first.

We are getting on with the programmes for the three concerts, and I hope to send a draft for your approval fairly soon.

Yrs ever
Adrian

Elgar accepted the challenge, shaping his work especially for the medium of recording and broadcasting, as Boult was to point out in a lecture at the Royal Institution:

I remember years ago a distinguished musician pointing out to me that the actual sound given by an early Beethoven or a Haydn Symphony seemed more intense and brilliant than the sound made by a much larger orchestra in a work, say, by Tchaikowsky or Richard Strauss. The reason for this is, I think, that the smaller orchestra with its more open chording enables the harmonies of the instruments to be heard much more clearly than when they are obscured by duplication by some other instrument of a different quality. This factor was recently recognised by Sir Edward Elgar who, in re-scoring Chopin's Funeral March specially for gramophone reproduction, took pains to keep a very open and clear score and resisted the temptation of adding too much to the richness and thickness of the texture.[1]

When the recording was made by Boult with the B.B.C. Symphony Orchestra at E.M.I.'s new Abbey Road Studios on 30th May, Elgar and his daughter came up from Worcester for the session. That day made a beginning for another and far bigger creative project when Elgar was approached by the critic Ferruccio Bonavia, who was later to write:

When I saw Elgar some time ago supervising the recording of his admirable orchestrated version of Chopin's Funeral March I ventured to express the hope that he would complete the work thus begun and score the other movements of the Sonata, which would then become a symphony. Elgar demurred, pointing out the difficulties of scoring the last movement, difficulties, which, I know, he alone could completely overcome. He concluded by saying that he would rather write a symphony of his own.

It seemed a hint that the composer whose music had fallen silent at his wife's death a dozen years earlier would like to get back to work. That hint was to produce extraordinary action in the months ahead.

Planning a holiday in Italy that summer, Boult had a typical send-off from Sir Hugh Allen:

[1] Reprinted in *The Listener*, 28th December 1932, p. 946.

Royal College of Music,
Prince Consort Road,
South Kensington, London S.W.7.
1 June 1932

My dear Adrian

You will be interested to know that when I was in Brussels talking at dinner with all kinds of musicians from France & Germany they considered the BBC orchestra was the best broadcaster in Europe.

When you come back from the sunshine of Italy I want you to give Jacques some odd lessons in conducting so that he may with the minimum of athleticism get the maximum of spiritual effect (Walford D).

Is it possible?

Go & stew in the sun & God be with you.

Yrs ever H.P.A.

On 1st December 1932 Boult stood in for Donald Tovey to conduct a concert with the Reid Symphony Orchestra in Edinburgh. The programme (with notes by Tovey) included Haydn's Symphony no. 95, the Walton Viola Concerto with Lionel Tertis and extracts from Glazunov's *Scènes de ballet* op. 52. When the audience showed insufficient appreciation of the Walton Concerto, Boult turned round and announced they should have it again. And so they did, at the expense of the Glazunov later in the programme.

Hedenham Lodge, Bungay, Suffolk.
Dec. 3 1932

Dear Adrian

Repeating the Walton was a splendid idea. I should like to think that I might have had the gumption to do it if I had been there. It's the sort of thing that ought to happen. I hope the audience took it well the 2nd time. The broadcast reached me here in patches which sufficed to shew that the first performance was very good. But I notice, making every allowance for familiarity, that classical harmony & scoring are quite unmistakably more transmissible than things remoter from them. The Haydn sounded twice as loud as anything else. I'm glad I was wrong about lengths & that (except for dear old

Glazy whom I'll put into a later programme) you were able to stick to the right order of events.

Many thanks for all you've done for us
                    Yours ever
                    Donald Francis Tovey

In the autumn came the three Elgar 75th birthday concerts. The programmes finally arranged with the B.B.C. Symphony Orchestra for performance in Queen's Hall and simultaneous broadcast were:

30th November. *Cockaigne Overture*, conducted by Elgar
              Violin Concerto (Albert Sammons, conducted by Elgar)
              First Symphony (conducted by Sir Landon Ronald)

7th December. *Introduction and Allegro* (conducted by Boult)
             'Enigma' Variations (conducted by Boult)
             Second Symphony (conducted by Elgar)

14th December. *The Kingdom* (with B.B.C. Chorus) (conducted by Boult).

A week before the first concert Elgar sent a letter of performing suggestions for the First Symphony.

Marl Bank, Worcester.
22nd November 1932.

My dear Adrian,

I do not want to worry you unduly but perhaps one of your assistants could see to the following matter, *if* you approve of my suggestion. In the first Symphony there are some passages which I have never got to my liking. In the passage beginning four bars before ☐30 (and occurring twice more) I want an *echo* effect, – the only thing to be *heard* in the first two bars being the *quaver passage* (Clar, Cello, Viola, Vl.II.) which should be slurred right over and the solo violin really *pp*.

Would you allow some one to mark the copies, one (or two) desks only to play?

These are the 'spots'. Begin four bars before ☐30, – 'Echo' four bars; at ☐30 *tutti* for four bars: then Echo eight bars. (NB. Vio.I (tutti) come in at the end of bar 8.)

Again, the same sort of thing at ☐53 ; Echo, four bars; – piu lento, tutti two bars; – then Echo six bars; – allargando, *tutti*.

105

I am looking forward keenly to seeing you again and hearing this symphony with your gorgeous orchestra.

Ever yours,

Edward Elgar

. . . At the last rehearsal [for *The Kingdom*] he twice said 'Don't let them go away, Adrian. I want to come and speak to them when you have finished.' He came on to the platform and gave a most moving and charming speech of thanks to them for their support and friendship all his life.[1]

During the final concert it was announced that the B.B.C. had commissioned Elgar's Third Symphony, on which the old man would start work immediately.

Broadcasting House, London, W.1.
15/12/32

Dear Sir Edward –
It is nearly as hopeless to try & write, as to try & speak all the things that we all – & I most particularly – have felt during these great weeks. It has been a *great* experience for all of us, & I know how the whole orchestra has – we all have – been thrilled by it.

And the greatest part of it is to think that another Symphony is coming, & coming in the autumn. I had no idea until I saw the paper this morning that it was already so far advanced. It will indeed make next Season a 'peak'.

Many many thanks for your splendid help – I wish we could start all over again, & I would try & do better justice to my part of it.

Yours always

Adrian

Marl Bank, Rainbow Hill, Worcester
30th December 1932.

My dear Adrian,
I am now at home and able to write concerning the three

---

[1] 'I knew Edward Elgar', in *London calling*, July 12th 1951, p. 13.

Concerts which the B.B.C. did me the honour to give in November and December.

It is impossible for me to convey exactly what I wish you and all of your colleagues to understand regarding the splendid performances of my things. My gratitude to everyone concerned is unbounded and I shall be greatly indebted to you if you will find some means to let the members of the chorus, the orchestra and the soloists know my appreciation of their wholehearted sympathy and support.

To you, my dear Adrian, I will say that the renewal of the atmosphere of the Second Symphony at the People's Palace under your direction was one of the happiest events of my life and I thank you.

With warm regards,
I am your affectionate friend,
Edward Elgar

Broadcasting House, London, W.1.
11/1/33

Dear Sir Edward,

Your *very* kind letter reached me just as I was starting home, & cheered my journey very much. I shall certainly let the choir & orchestra all hear what you have said about them, & they will be proud & touched. We all felt it was a rare honour to play our parts in the concerts, and are indeed happy that you should have been satisfied.

We now look forward with the keenest interest to the grand concert of next season, & feel confident that the third Symphony will take its place with the other two, & most proud that the B.B.C. orchestra will be the first to produce it.

With very many thanks
Yours always
Adrian

Elgar had not begun his Symphony before Vaughan Williams finished his Piano Concerto, and sent in the score to Boult.

The White Gates, Westcott Road, Dorking.
[undated, received at B.B.C. 3rd January 1933]

Dear Adrian

I hope very much to be at the rehearsal on *Monday* – but I may possibly be prevented –

Now what I am frightened about in this Concerto is the *balance* [–] it may be *overscored* – so if I am not there I give you *carte blanche* to thin out the score as you wish if you do not think the pfte will come through enough (it is necessarily *right on the top* all the way through)

I hope Gustav will be at the rehearsal

        Yrs
        R Vaughan Williams

P.S. At all events you very likely won't want all the desks of strings playing all the time.

After the Concerto's première on 1st February and a party given by Vaughan Williams's sister-in-law, he wrote his thanks.

The White Gates, Westcott Road, Dorking.
February 7 1933

Dear Adrian

I have now sufficiently recovered from the shock of last Wednesday to be able to write to thank you and your orchestra for your beautiful performance. You have made impossible the composer's time-honoured excuse that the work would have sounded all right if it had been properly played – I could not have imagined a better performance.

I am so sorry that you were not at Mrs. Fisher's party after the concert. Some of the guests were invited by me and some by her and we both took it for granted that you were the first person who would be invited by the other. When we discovered our mistake we telephoned wildly to every conceivable address, but in vain –

        Yrs
        R Vaughan Williams

From the continent later in the year came a letter of thanks from Artur Schnabel – together with some early evidence of the Nazi menace.

Villa Ginetta, Tremezzo (Lago di Como)
6th June, 33

Dear Dr. Boult,
   Many thanks for your two letters. The performances with you, last season, I shall not forget. The work your wonderful orchestra is doing stands out by its union of noblesse and vigour, warmth and simplicity, virtuosity and reverence. How astonishing such achievements in a few years! England can be congratulated for that model institution (and envied too). My son[1] is most grateful for the interest you take in him. He will write soon to let you know the dates he has in England.
   I have not yet given up the hope that the endeavour to get some activity for Doctor Fritz Stiedry will finally be successful. He would have deserved it always to be invited but in his present situation it seems to me almost an obligation to show him that a good artist is not yet lost in a desert when he, in sheerest innocence, has been condemned to idleness by political measures with which he never had anything to do and which certainly no intelligent person can understand. So will you excuse me, if I am asking you again not to forget him.
   I have written to Mr. Bromley.[2] I think he will come here in July to have some lessons with me.
   Now with kindest regards
                    yours very sincerely
                    Artur Schnabel

The summer holiday that year made a difference.
   On 1 July 1933 he married. The honeymoon of Adrian and Ann Boult was enriched by the wedding gift of Gustav Holst – a manuscript sealed and marked 'To be opened in Italy and not before'. It was a canon he had written specially for them to Marlowe's verses 'Come live with me and be my love'.

[1] Karl Ulrich Schnabel.   [2] Thomas Bromley, a young pianist from Birmingham.

A Canon
for A and A from Gst
for use in Steiny, King's Langley, Gregynog and other nice places.

At the end of the honeymoon there was this note:

St. Paul's Girls' School, Brook Green, Hammersmith, W.6.
July 31 [1933]

Dear Adrian
  I) Welcome Home
  II) My love to your old Dutch
  III) And tell her from me to lead you astray so that you forget as many duties as possible.
  IV) If you honour me by doing my Choral Symphony I want you to have a free hand. But the more I think of it the more I want D[orothy] Silk.

Yr
G

PS V) When are you two going to sing my latest op to me?

Further Holst broadcasts were planned for the 1933–34 season. Other British composers were also honoured. Among them was Sir Walford Davies, whose *Everyman* (written for the Leeds Festival of 1904) was revived in a broadcast performance by Boult on 15th October 1933.

High Meadow, Cookham Dean, Berks.
16.x.33

Dearest Adrian,
  It was simply lovely of you to take all that good care of old Everyman. You would have been pleased with the transmission as we got it here. The 'Chamber music' conception of the orchestral accompaniment came right across, and made for the first time in my 30 years experience of it since Leeds (and of course including Leeds itself) a wholly intimate thing of it, with just the near intimacy that I had longed for and thought so easy. It was in fact literally its 'first performance'.
  I long to begin to write at that point shunning its inefficiencies and overdone messes, which did not seem so insuperable. Thank you, thank you, thank you ⸺

Yours
W

But the great centrepiece of the year, Elgar's Third Symphony, was doomed by the sudden illness of the old composer. He lingered for several months. In December there seemed an improvement, and Boult allowed himself to hope along with everyone else.

8 Chelsea Embankment, S.W.3.
16/12/33

Dear Sir Edward,
It is splendid to hear from Landon [Ronald] that you are now getting well again. I have had news of you from time to time from Scott [Sunderland] & Barry [Jackson] & as I see no lights in their flat tonight I expect they are [at] Malvern for the weekend & will bring more news on Monday.
With much love & good wishes for a quick & complete recovery,
Yours always
Adrian

Back came a last post card, dictated to a secretary but signed at the end with a shaky signature.

Nursing Home, Worcester,
18th December 1933
Dictated.

My dear Adrian,
Thank you very much for your note and good wishes. I fear my friends are unduly optimistic; the announcement of my return home was a mistake and I fear it will be a considerable time before this can happen.
My love to you
Yours ever,
signed: – Edward Elgar

On 23rd February 1934 he died – to be followed a few months later by Delius.

Three weeks after Elgar's death Boult conducted the English première of Alban Berg's *Wozzeck* at a Queen's Hall concert sponsored and broadcast by the B.B.C. The broadcast reached the composer, who wrote next day from Austria:

Waldhaus, Auen am Worthersee
15.3.34

Dear Mr. Boult,[1]

I am longing to tell you how yesterday's *Wozzeck* performance delighted me. In the relay from Sottens (Geneva) I heard *clearly*, and so I can judge on how high an artistic level and with what rare success the performance went forward. But I can also measure – as no one else could – what an immense preparation must have preceded this concert. It equalled the finest stage-performances with the work in the regular repertory. And so I must tell you of the one thing in this performance which did *not* please me but made me sad: that this immense amount of work, perseverance, talent and genius – in a word, that such great *love* for one work (without which such success would never have been possible) – was put together only for this *one* performance, to remain only in memory when the last chord had died away.

But, turning from this all too understandable phenomenon of concert-performance, it gives me only joy and happiness to think of the performance – and to think long of it. The greatest happiness of all, perhaps, is the implied *understanding* with which this (one might say) up to then strange music was revealed. That is owing first of all to *you*, dear Mr. Boult, and your strong shaping revealed through the whole performance; but then to your unique *orchestra*, and to the musically and vocally outstanding *singers*. And on these *last* the emphasis should be placed. It was only a *single* performance, and there one is accustomed (as a middle-European) to the usual concert-oratorio singing style. But what emerged *here* under your sovereign direction was a performance as if from the regular repertory of the greatest stage! And that is one accomplishment which – as I have cause to know from 2 or 3 dozen *Wozzeck*-productions – appears very seldom.

Let me thank you, dear Mr. Boult, most profoundly for this! Please give my thanks to all – really to *all* your wonderful performers, and say that I wish I could send a letter of thanks

[1] Translated from German.

113

to each and every one of them – that I thank only you because I know only your name.*

Now I greet you, Mr. Boult, (to know you personally now would make me really happy) with gratitude as your true admirer.

Alban Berg

* May I request a copy of the programme?

Further broadcasts were planned to include music by Holst – his *Choral Symphony* and a new Lyric Movement for viola and orchestra which Lionel Tertis was to play in its first performance with the B.B.C. Symphony Orchestra on 18th March. Early in the month Holst sent a long letter about these works to Mrs. Beckett. But there was bad news of himself: he had been in hospital.

St. Paul's Girls' School,
Brook Green, Hammersmith, W.6.
(I am sorry I forgot to tell you that this is my address again)
March 5 [1934]

Dear Mrs Beckett

I was just going to write a long letter to Dr Boult when your kind one arrived so I'll live up to my principles and B[other] M[rs] B[eckett].

Would you thank the gentleman who sent me the three tickets for each of the rehearsals and the performance on March 18. Could I have the same number again?

Would you tell Mr Lord that I regret I cannot write the program notes for my choral symphony. I'm not the man for that job because I hate all explanations of music unless I've heard the music beforehand (because they can't do any harm then). Mr Tertis is writing the note for the viola piece on March 18 and is leaving out the only important point which is that it is written for and dedicated to him!

Could I have the score and parts of the viola piece (Lyric movement) for a few days in order to make a slight alteration. If this is not convenient I enclose a sketch of the bar to be changed. It is the second bar of the Poco Animato in E major (only the first three beats in the violins and violas are altered).

114

If Dr Boult wants the score would you get this little alteration made in score and parts and let me have the bill?

I am so sorry I never told him that I left the Clinic ten days ago unhealed. The doctors there wanted me to be operated on at once as they said I was in such good condition. I did not feel so at all and felt and still feel much disappointed and quite cross. I have gone back to my regular doctor who is a sensible unpretentious GP. But he feels that as medicine has failed I ought to try surgery. A year ago I wanted to (he was against it then) because I thought that surgery was a matter of kill or cure and I'm all for that. But now they tell me that at my age the only really useful operation would take me probably a year to get over!!! So I've warned my GP that I'm thinking of trying quacks and he has promised not to be stuffy. But for the next week or so I want to try and lead a quiet normal life and to think things over and to lose my bad temper!

In answer to your two queries, I would love to be 'worried' – which usually means 'interested' – about work and am thinking most definitely about consulting Sir John Weir. I've no brains for spoiling music paper yet and am not allowed to wag a stick so Misses Day and Lasker do the latter for me when I teach and the nearest I get to the former is to correct extremely badly copied parts.

Also I – as you may notice – have taken to writing very long letters.

Ys Sincerely
Gustav Holst

But when the time came for the rehearsals and broadcast première of his *Lyric Movement*, Holst was too ill to be present. On the day before the performance he sent this note:

2 Elm Cresc [Ealing]
Saturday [17th March 1934]

Dear Adrian

You and Tertis are to have an absolutely free hand over my new thing. Just do what you like with it. And accept my thanks

115

in advance, also my blessing. And the same to L[ionel] T[ertis] and the other players.

Ys Ever
Gustav

I shall listen in tomorrow

It was almost a valediction, for Holst died on 25th May. Two months later came a letter from his greatest friend, Vaughan Williams.

The White Gates, Westcott Road, Dorking.
[27th July 1934]

Dear Adrian

Several people have expressed surprize to me that the Proms contain no concert devoted to Gustav's music – I have an idea that one of the B.B.C. Autumn Concerts is going to be devoted to his music – am I right in this? and if so may I tell people who ask me why there is no Concert of his music at the 'Proms'?

Also you may know that Gustav was planning a Symphony of which the Scherzo was already finished. I feel this ought to have an important place in next season's scheme – *not* at a memorial concert (as a sort of pious memorial) but for its own sake at an ordinary concert.

Will it fit in to one of the B.B.C. Wednesdays or shall I write to the Philharmonic?

Yrs
RVW

The British Broadcasting Corporation
Broadcasting House, London, W.1.
16th August 1934

Dear Ralph,

I am sorry we have been so long answering your letter, particularly as I gather you want the information for other people.

Various circumstances, which are too long to write, but which I will tell you, have made it only possible that our second Concert should contain a memorial to Gustav. We are doing *The Planets* that day, and I hope it will be a worthy performance. Owing to the previous engagement of Myra Hess, who can come on no other date, it is not possible to give the complete programme to his works, but a space is being left in a later Concert for the Scherzo. We certainly should like to have it, though I am always careful to say that we are not out to grasp first performances. If it is of use to other organisations to have the first performance, we are quite content to give the second. This is a matter of principle, but I personally do feel rather selfish and greedy where the Scherzo is concerned.

One of our Programme Advisory Committee members mentioned a new Symphony by yourself. I need hardly say we are only too ready to get more information when you feel like giving it to us.

Yours ever,
Adrian

Boult and the B.B.C. Symphony gave the first performance of Holst's Scherzo on 6th February 1935. Two months later, on 10th April, they played the première of Vaughan Williams's Symphony in F minor. The composer sent a fulsome tribute. Then came the question of whether to take the new Symphony to Salzburg – where Boult was to conduct the Vienna Philharmonic – or to give *Job*, which had now been dedicated to Boult. Vaughan Williams had definite ideas about that and the rest of the Salzburg programme as well.

The White Gates, Westcott Road, Dorking.
April 14 [1935]

Dear Adrian

On the whole I prefer *Job*. For one thing I want to make a few slight revisions in the Symph and would therefore like, if the occasion arises, to hear it again in England before we shove it off on the foreigners.

Also, I feel that *Job* is less like what they are accustomed to, which I feel is what we ought to give them – but do as you like *really* – These considerations are not important.

117

I am not quite happy about the rest of the programme – but I daresay that is inevitable. Could you not do Bax 3rd Symphony instead of *Tintagel* – and *The P[erfect] F[ool]* Ballet or *Egdon Heath* or *Hammersmith* [by Holst] instead of the Fugal Overture – which is not one of my favourite works.

Yrs
RVW

The British Broadcasting Corporation,
Broadcasting House, London, W.1.
22/4/35.

Dear Ralph,

It was great to get your letter, because I know you aren't given to exaggerating. And my delay in answering isn't because I was slack but just *very* rushed.

I think you saw what we all felt about the Symphony – if there was an inspiration about the performance it was the *work* that put it there. And if I got the bit between my teeth it was simply because the music made me feel like that. You know I feel that it is all very well for conductors to have their readings when works have taken their place in the repertory. While they are new it is *really* his business to absorb the composer's mind as much as possible – his own will emerge later; in fact, all too soon usually. And though it is harder perhaps (different anyway), I feel there is no excuse for a conductor who, at a first performance, causes a composer to say 'Very interesting, perhaps, but not my work.' In R.C.M. days we spent most of our time on conducting accompaniments – I always used to say it was easy to do symphonies. So don't worry if I ask too many questions – the thing will shake down after a performance or two – & then you may cease to recognise it!

I do agree about [Holst's] *P[erfect] F[ool]* at Salzburg & will do it if ① there is time ② we can rehearse enough. Re Bax I am more hard hearted – they know so little of him that small doses won't matter perhaps at first. And a Symphony to start with is pretty strong meat. *Job* certainly – I wish there were time for both!

118

See you at Dorking – good luck to it all – & *many* thanks for the letter *and* the symphony.

> Yrs ever
> Adrian.

Boult's Salzburg programme included the first performance of Bliss's *Music for strings*, Bax's *Tintagel*, Holst's *Perfect Fool* Ballet, and *Job*.

Broadcasts and concerts in Europe were taking Boult's fame abroad. He became the object of 'fan' mail.

Lisbon, 19th. February 1935

Dear Sir

All weeks I read English programs in order to see simphonic concerts to hear.

What lovely music sometimes I can listen, chiefly when are you the conductor of this fantastic B.B.C. Orchestra.

Hearing the public enthusiasm in Queen's Hall, I wished be present also, showing my admiration.

What enthusiasm can communicate at distance your vehement interpretation.

I never will forget your manner in the first simphony of Brahms and in the 5th. of Beethoven, so old but in your hands so young.

Unhappily in Portugal, if I can hear I cannot see and it is still the cruel sorrow of the T.S.F.

So I wonder your art, that I beg in order to see you nearly one photography of you, with your autograph.

I think that I am the first Portuguese, who begs you this attention, but I am certain that you have here many admirators.

And this will give mee, more pleasure that all fotos of Hollywood.

I thank you very much previously, and I am always in this country at your orders.

> Your faithfully
> Alfredo Rodrigues Ferreira

119

And for musicians in an increasingly troubled world, Boult was a figurehead of all that was sane and permanent. One of the distinguished players displaced by the rise of Nazism was Carl Flesch.

65. Gloucester Place,
London, W.1.
27.3.'36

Dear Dr. Boult,
Thanks for your letter of March. 25th. After what you have said about Mr. Berkeley Mason I shall of course be glad to play with him. I am writing him by the same mail. May I take the opportunity to congratulate you on your splendid performance of the ninth, to which I listened in. It was one of the most sincere and accomplished renditions I ever heard.
With kindest regards
Yours sincerely
Carl Flesch

It will certainly interest you, that the Home Office has granted me a permanent and unrestricted labor-permit in this country, so that we decided to settle here definitely.

A short spring tour with the B.B.C. Orchestra on the continent brought the first public performance in Vienna of Schönberg's *Variations* op. 31. The composer was not there, but one of his most popular contemporaries was – Franz Lehar.

Vienna
23rd April 1936.

Dear Doctor:[1]
Permit me to congratulate you from the heart on today's great success.

I wanted to greet you in the artists' room during the interval, but you were so surrounded that I could not get to you.

So I take this way to thank you deeply as an artist for the great occasion you have brought to us.

[1] Translated from German.

It will remain for me an unforgettable evening.
With special regards,
                    Your admirer
                    Fz Lehár

The beginning of a new season at home brought a performance of Vaughan Williams's *Sea Symphony* with Noel Eadie, William Parsons, and the B.B.C Chorus and Orchestra. On the following day the composer made his tribute an evaluation of Boult's art.

The White Gates, Westcott Road, Dorking.
[22nd October 1936]
(n.d., but bears Mrs. Beckett's pencilled note of 23.10.36)

Dear Adrian
    There seem to me to be two essentials of great conducting
(1) Faithfulness to the composer
(2) The power of the conductor to express *himself* to the full *at the moment* – to feel himself in the music & the music in himself. I always know I shall get (1) from you but sometimes without (2). Thank heaven I have never heard from you (2) without (1) – & I know I never shall.
    Yesterday we had (1) + (2) – result a great performance & great conducting for which I thank you from the bottom of my heart – and your singers & players too – the chorus were superb – their sincerity, their words, their tone, their phrasing
    The orchestra I knew wd be magnificent – even our friend the 1st. Oboe, who seemed to have swallowed a dose of vinegar before the Mozart had evidently corrected it with something more delectable during the interval.
    – You made me like the old work again & the awkward places seemed to have disappeared by magic.
    Things that stick out particularly in my memory are the end of the slow movement, the scherzo & the beginning and end of the 'Explorers' – though it was really all 'high lights'
    – Just to show that this is not just undiscriminating praise I was occasionally disappointed in the soloists (partly owing I think to my position) – but the duet in No IV was wonderful

even the tiresome man in front of me who was getting bored and fidgetty – hushed down to attention during that.

Thank you again 1000 times,

R V W

Of the oboeist Boult himself recalled another occasion:

. . . One of the older players, whose taste in drink was on the strong side, was seized with a coughing fit. Somebody got him some water, and this was passed over as I went on with the rehearsal. Gradually I became more and more conscious of disturbance, so I stopped and shouted: 'What *is* the matter? Haven't you ever seen a man drink a glass of water before?'

'*Not that man!*' came the response in perfect unison.[1]

The Coronation year Honours were to contain the announcement of Boult's knighthood. In advance came this letter from the B.B.C. Director General, Sir John Reith, addressed to Boult's wife.

Broadcasting House, London, W.1.
Feb.1.1937.

Dear Mrs. Boult,

I do hope you are satisfied that the right thing was done & the right conclusions come to by yourself and Himself (as we say in the North).

Anyhow the news has given great pleasure here, and I am sure elsewhere as well. I hope very much that you will both enjoy that part of it – the satisfaction given to all your friends.

Please don't bother to acknowledge this.

Yours very sincerely,

J. C. W. Reith.

As Sir Adrian he would conduct the Coronation Service for King George VI and Queen Elizabeth in June. Normal duties and engagements crowded round. In the spring of 1937 he was to conduct the first gramophone recording of *Music for Strings* by Arthur Bliss. The composer was closely involved. One of his tasks was to accommodate the side-breaks necessary for 78-rpm recording.

---

[1] *My own trumpet*, p. 108.

East Heath Lodge, 1 East Heath Road, Hampstead, N.W.3.
April 10th [1937]

Dear Adrian.

I have divided Music for Strings into six sides comfortably so that you need not rush either the Slow movement or the end of the first movement. I enclose them. I shall have the times of them accurately for you on Friday morning, if we are recording it then.

I hope so, otherwise I see it shelved.

... Yours ever
Arthur.

In the event the recording was postponed, but only until 25th June. A month later Bliss had received test pressings.

East Heath Lodge, 1 East Heath Road, Hampstead, N.W.3.
July 29th [1937]

Dear Adrian.

I listened to the recordings of *Music for Strings* this morning. It is a lovely performance and I thank you very much indeed. You do not know what a joy it is to know that an authentic model of performance is now on record. I do not suppose Ann's & your holidays will bring you west Pen Pitwards – but it would be grand to catch a glimpse of you between Aug 1st – Sept 30th when we shall be there

With all kind messages to you both
Arthur.

On 29th June Boult had directed the première of Howard Ferguson's *Partita*. A second performance in February 1938 brought a grateful letter from the composer.

34, Willoughby Road, Hampstead, N.W.3.
21.II.38

Dear Adrian,

Thank you very much for the fine performance you gave of my *Partita* last night, and for all the trouble you took over it; in spite of your saying 'that's what we are here for', I still maintain that there are not many people who would go so

123

whole heartedly after what the composer is trying to get at. Afterwards, when you asked me about tempi, I felt it was rather churlish to say that the last movement was a fraction slow. Such a point might be felt by the unduly sensitive parent of the 'child' – who after all has a wholly impossible standard of values – but would not, I am convinced, be noticed by anybody else. Forget it, therefore, and think of the work as *you* feel it must go. This will be much more likely to produce what we both want than if you bother yourself over the split-hair differences noticed by your troublesome but very grateful friend,

Howard.

No answer please! I know how many letters you have to cope with.

Another performance of Bliss's *Music for Strings* during the B.B.C. Orchestra's visit to Plymouth on 20th April 1938 brought a different kind of appreciation from Arthur Bliss.

Pen Pits, Pen Selwood, Bourton, Dorset.
Thursday

Many thanks, dear Adrian, for your breath taking performance of Music for Strings. Listening to such magnificent playing gives me the greatest impetus to go on developing my talent to something better

As ever your
Arthur.

Among conducting colleagues, the oldest relations were with Bruno Walter. They had begun in Munich in 1912, when the 23-year-old Boult saw his first three Mozart opera performances directed by Walter:

They were *Don Giovanni*, *Cosi*, and *Figaro* in the exquisite little Residenztheater, unaltered since Mozart had conducted *Idomeneo* in it in 1788. The new Director had certainly got into his stride; I didn't suppose I should ever hear Mozart performances of such all-round perfection, and certainly I never have again.[1]

[1] *My own trumpet*, p. 31.

A decade later he met Walter in Munich, and there began an acquaintance which was slowly to blossom. In the Birmingham appointment, Walter was one of the first guest conductors he invited, and the pattern was carried on at the B.B.C. But what brought this friendship to its maturity was not music at all but the menace of political events. Now conducting the Vienna Philharmonic, Walter's life in Vienna was one of the first victims of the Anschluss early in 1938. In answer to Boult's sympathy and concern came the following:

Hotel Hermitage, Monte-Carlo
21.3.1938

My dear Friend!

I thank you of all my heart for your dear words. I know that you feel with me and that you understand – better than anybody else – what besides my personal sufferances the death of Austria means to all of us.

It is indeed tragic beyond belief and it is a difficult task to adapt oneself to this new Europe. I had in the Hague a delightful conversation with Mr. Owen Mase[1] – it was a real comfort for me to feel his sympathy and full understanding for the happenings of last week. – Once more thousand thanks and my love to you and Lady Boult

In friendship yours
Bruno Walter

Hotel Hermitage, Monte-Carlo
30.3.1938

My dear friend!

In grateful remembrance of the sympathy you have shown me I want to tell you that a great sorrow has been taken from me: my daughter is again free (since two days) and we hope to see her here or in Switzerland as soon as the frontiers will be open again for people with Austrian passports. I know you

---

[1] Boult's assistant at the B.B.C.

take part in my affairs and so I felt I must tell you also about these good news.

Kindest greetings to you and Lady Boult
always yours in friendship
Bruno Walter

La Pace – Grand Hotel, Montecatini Terme
12.6.1938

My dear friend!

I thank you thousand times for your dear letter – it was entirely and genuinely Adrian Boult (a good criticism, be sure). I got it here, where I am making the cure, after a most strenuous time in Paris and in Florence. I made up my mind to take a good rest – the possibility of which belongs to the rather few advantages brought about by the happenings of the last months. My daughter Lotte is at this moment in Lugano in Switzerland with her sister: and my wife and I, we will join our children and my younger daughter's husband end of this month there.

My next season is 'sold out' except March which I reserved for America – but it is still doubtful if the negotiations will lead to a positive result. I would regret if I would not go, for I am absolutely of your opinion: Europe is bad and darker and darker are the clouds hanging over our heads. I am glad in the thought, to come again to England and make some music there and let me hope to see you there – it would do me so good to have a 'heart to heart talk' with you, to be again with you for some time: our personal life is not less important for us than our artistic life – perhaps even more. And we, slaves of our work, let it pass and remain the losers in the play. My best love to you and Lady Boult – always yours in friendship

Bruno Walter

My wife joins me in my greetings.

On the brink of the Second World War came a last gesture for peace – a World's Fair at New York in the summer of 1939. Boult went over to conduct two all-British programmes in Carnegie Hall with the New York Philharmonic-Symphony Orchestra. Leon

Goossens played his brother Eugene's Oboe Concerto, and there were three premières: Vaughan Williams's *Five Variants on 'Dives and Lazarus'*, Arnold Bax's Seventh Symphony, and a Piano Concerto by Arthur Bliss, dedicated 'To the People of the United States of America', in which the soloist was Solomon.

The Second World War came irresistibly forward. Its darkest days brought the reflections of Bruno Walter from the United States.

910 Bedford Drive, Beverly Hills, California
17.6.1940

My dear Adrian!

Nothing could give me a greater joy than your very dear letter. I am thinking of you so often, my dear friend, and of your dear family and I am thinking of all my good friends over there and of grand old England – with a longing to be with you and to share what you have to go through. I feel guilty to live here the sheltered life of peace while you have to face this onslaught of hell. You cannot imagine how terrible it is to be so far of all one loves and to live in the spirit with all the agony this noble France had to suffer – and will have to suffer. Well, also this country is preparing vigorously for all the looming possibilities for it seems the visions of the Apocalypse come true and the power of evil are unchained against humanity regardless of countries. – It was so comforting for me to see by your program that you carry on and feed the hearts of the people with music whenever the roar of hell permits to listen to sounds from the spritual world. I personally am fighting the battle between the horrors of reality and the powers which have dominated my whole life in myself every day. I try to write a book, a musician's book, always interrupted by sorrow and grief and anxiety and always clinging again to the thoughts and feelings to which I belong by nature.* – My dear friend I only would be too happy to come back and conduct again at the B.B.C. and be sure I have no other wish than to return as soon as it can be with safety for my wife and daughter. – I think back with such pleasure and gratitude to our last charming afternoon and evening with you and your family at your country-house and I think back with deep emotions to my last beautiful contacts with your excellent orchestra and chorus. Please give my love to all of them, to all the dear friends in England – I am with you with all my wishes and thoughts. Let us keep in touch and write again soon. Yours ever in friendship

Bruno

* I shall conduct concerts in the Hollywood Bowl and in November and December in Los Angeles and in January and February in New York. No plans afterwards until now.

The B.B.C. Orchestra had been evacuated to Bristol. A broadcast performance of Bax's Seventh Symphony made a memorable contrast to everyday events in 1940 when it reached the composer:

The Rising Sun Hotel, Lynmouth, N. Devon.
June 21st. 5.30 [1940]

My dear Adrian

I must write immediately to congratulate upon and thank you for the very clear and vital rendering of my symphony this afternoon. I was particularly moved by the playing of the Second movement which expressed all the heavy summer languor which I meant it to convey. In the record sent me from America this movement was a little too easy-going, but the *tempi* to-day were quite perfect.

Many thanks indeed for a most enjoyable experience – rather a strange one too, for I have heard practically no music at all since the war began, and like almost every composer have been totally unable to do any creative work at all.

My best wishes.

Yours ever,
Arnold.

The details of programme-planning continued exacting as ever. A programme submitted for broadcast by Myra Hess brought this letter from Boult:

'The conductor speaks':
an early BBC television
programme from the
Alexandra Palace,
14th May 1939

Photo: BBC

Photo: Georg Schenker

Conducting the Vienna Symphony Orchestra, 26th March 1947

Recording the Vaughan Williams Symphonies, Kingsway Hall,
December 1953: Adrian Boult with Ursula and Ralph
Vaughan Williams

Listening to tapes at the EMI Studios, 1978. In the past fourteen
years Sir Adrian has made over sixty recordings with Christopher Bishop,
producer (*left*) and Christopher Parker, balance engineer

Photo: David Farrell

'To dearest Adrian with devoted love from his no-longer-so-young
colleague Yehudi, November 7, 1962'

Bristol,
29th June, 1940

Dear Myra,

A letter from Ibbs and Tillett about your next broadcast recital on 1st August has arrived in my office, and I see that you would like to play Howard Ferguson's Sonata. As you will probably hear through Miss Bass that we do not feel able to take the work in this position in programmes, I should like to explain to you the significance of the 8.0. to 8.30 period at which your recital is fixed.

This is known as a 'star recital', and our programme direction requires that we place there not only a 'star' artist, but also a programme which will have the widest possible appeal to the larger number of music-lovers. Do not for a moment imagine that in this case there is any reflection intended on Ferguson's music – as proof of that I may tell you that a few days later, on 4th August, we are including his violin and piano sonata played by himself and Isolde Menges. So I hope very much that you will be able to find a programme which will both please you and, also, fit our needs.

> Yours ever
> Adrian

48, Wildwood Road, N.W.11.
July 4th 1940

Dear Adrian

It was nice of you to write – I quite understand about the Ferguson Sonata – but I do hope it can be placed as a 'non-star-turn'?! some time – It makes a deep impression wherever I play it.

I would give a great deal to be able to broadcast from London (as opposed to somewhere outside it) on August 1st. – Is there any possibility of my being allowed to? Howardie has been called up – & my work at the N[ational] Gallery is going to be terrific without him – & I would gladly forgo the uncertainties of travelling. Don't give it another thought if it is impossible – or even too difficult –

I think of you all – & pray for your safety –
                With love
                Myra

The private correspondence with Bruno Walter went on.

910 North Bedford Drive, Beverly Hills, California
8.10.1940

My dear Adrian!

Nothing, really nothing could have given me so great pleasure, such deep satisfaction as your last letter. I even mentioned it and quoted it in a gathering for the Los Angeles Philharmonic, because it sets an example how a musician should feel in these times about his art and its eternal value. Of course until now (or short time ago) I would have preferred to find the people's minds here concentrated on England's fight, even to tell them that all spiritual values are at this moment of secondary importance because they only can survive by her victory. But now this country seems daily more awake, more conscious of the very meaning of this crusade – the hearts here are beating now with Britain's fame and now it seems advisable to make it clear to them that music matters even when bombs fall, that music is a strong Ally for the great cause by her direct influence on the human mind which means encouragement and moral help and after all: our spiritual world as well as our moral fundaments belong to the targets of the Nazi-guns and we have to preserve them for the new epoch of mankind, that will begin after this war. Never a nation has fought for a nobler, for a more important cause and Britain will have the spiritual and moral lead as well as the political one by her victory.

So you, my dear friend, are in fact in a marvellous position – you are entrusted with the task to carry out art unhurt, and undiminished in her meaning for your people, through this cataclysm. Your letter has shown me how conscious you are of the importance of your artistry and wholeheartedly I congratulate you on this attitude.

I am doing my best here to emphasise by artistry and by word the same opinion about art. For now of course the

130

world-happenings have begun to occupy the American mind. As I said before a drastic change is to be seen that makes me very happy and encourages me to make music with a clean conscience as help.

I read with much interest the book you sent me . . . the voice of the Nazi, which of course could not tell to me personally much new but has helped me to improve understanding in persons of importance. With real delight I saw your report about the Queenshall-entertainment – such happenings, so deeply British, are an incomparable means of spreading admiration and sympathy and should be reported here as much as possible. It warmed my heart to hear about the Bruckner-celebrations of which you wrote. Indeed, air-raids and Bruckner-Symphonies are a strange combination and I think your present life, so full of such contrasting experiences, must seem to you a romantic adventure in a new sense. I know too well, it is at the same time horror and tragedy but we must try and learn to rise above the feeling of being only the helpless victims of a cruel fate, to come nearer to the deeper sense of these happenings, to trust that their outcome will prove worth of the sacrifices and overhuman sufferances. By such growing understanding we get rid of the spiritual passivity of the mere object of destiny (you know Nietzsche's notion of 'amor fata') and this lesson should be learned now by all who still want to learn.

You will be interested to hear, that I have accepted an invitation of the Metropolitan Opera in New York and will conduct there as guest six weeks after my engagement with the New York Philharmonic. So I come back to Opera after three years purely Symphonic activity. My address will be the present one until end of December; and from January I shall be in New York, Hotel Dorset 30 West 54th Street. All good wishes to you, my dear friend. And believe me that I am with all my thoughts, day and night, with that grand old beloved country of yours. My warmest greetings to your dear wife and many greetings from my wife.

Always yours in friendship
Bruno

Then came an official request which Boult was asked to put to Vaughan Williams.

British Broadcasting Corporation, Bristol.
September 2nd 1940

Dr. Ralph

At the instigation of the Ministry of Information, the B.B.C. has asked me to approach you and ask you whether you would consider the acceptance of a commission to compose a 'Song or lay hymn' with orchestral accompaniment on a patriotic (but not necessarily war-time) theme; the lyric to be chosen by you from existing lyrics, or from poems which would be commissioned from certain living poets.

I won't enter at this point into further detail until I know whether you are interested enough to consider a proposal of this sort.

Needless to say, I very much hope you will be, as it is *you* we want.

Yours ever,
Adrian.

The White Gates, Dorking,
[no date]

Dear Adrian

I wish I'd known of this 6 months ago – because in a way I feel I've already shot my bolt & the M.O.I. are a day behind the fact – I shd love for the B.B.C. to have had the enclosed[1] which I think wd have just filled the bill – But as they did *not* ask me for anything I offered these to the Proms (who *did* ask me) & they are to be done on the 10th – Then the Bach Choir asked me & I refused them because I felt I had done all the occasional music I can – so if I do anything more it must be B.C. before B.B.C. – But perhaps a commission wd make me start writing which I feel quite incapable of at present.

So will you give me more details – I do not understand at present what you want.

[1] Six choral songs to be sung in time of war.

132

Is it (so to speak) the 'Jerusalem' brand or the 'Blest pair of sirens' brand which you want?

As regards verses I shall probably want to go to the old masters – But if the BBC like to send me any contemporary poems I wd consider them – but not promise to use them.

> Yrs
> R.V.W.

Soon it was agreed that Vaughan Williams should set William Ernest Henley's verses entitled *England, my England*.

The White Gates – Dorking
Oct 26 [1940]

Dear Adrian

Here is a suggestion for the patriotic song. Please criticize it

> (1) Its artistic merit if any
> (2) Its popularity & singability

It must hit the nail on the head and be able to be picked up by ear – For that reason I made it as square as possible – possibly to the detriment once or twice of its quality – for example in my original sketch line 2 ran –

What is there I would not do England my own.

Again at line 5 I originally had

Song on your bugles

but this seemed to me to pull it out too much – On the other hand is

'Song on your' too much of a quibble? In subsequent verses I have been obliged to make slight note alterations to fit the words but this is the case also in 'Jerusalem' which does not seem less singable on that account.

If you think this sketch is possible I would also suggest the following arrangement of Verses 1 & 2 Baritone Solo with chorus coming in at 'England'

Verse 3 Harmonized chorus
Verse 4 Everybody in unison with a descant – But as an alternative unison chorus throughout. Would you please pass this copy & letter on to Walford [Davies] for his criticism – I am also sending copies to Colles and [Hubert] Foss [at the Oxford University Press] for suggestions – Gustav used to say that he always asked for advice but never took it – I always say to my pupils that there are 3 things to do with advice (1) to reject it blindly – this is bad – (2) to accept it blindly – this is worse. (3) to let it sink in and suggest a 3rd course – this is good.

Yrs
RVW

P.S. Show it to any one you like for further opinions – Could not you get some of the more *un*musical of your staff together to try it over & see how well they picked it up!

Other perspectives on the war came from Bruno Walter, far away in a still peaceful United States.

Hotel Dorset, 30 West 54th Street, New York.
12.3.1941

My dear Adrian! It is several months ago that I wrote you my last letter and even your beautiful letter from the last days of November had to be unanswered until now – I was simply submerged with work and at present after having performed my last Opera at the Metropolitan (*Don Giovanni*) I feel like a swimmer who had dived for a long time and just comes up, water still in his eyes and streaming from his hair, fighting for breath. These months with the Philharmonic and later with the Metropolitan brought to a standstill everything except my musical work and so excuse me.

My heart and my mind have been, despite all this work, in England – all my wishes all my hopes center there and accordingly also my anxieties; but in fact without underrating the apocalyptic horrors Britain will still have to face and the mortal dangers for her shipping I am sure in the depth of my heart that she will come out of this battle for the good as

134

victorious as every better human being must hope for. I am happy here that finally the Lend Lease Bill has gone through; it will be of greatest importance and I am sure we will see now the whole of the U.S. working for the common cause (now it has been understood as the common cause). – I wrote a little article 'About war and music' that appeared in a new Magazine *Decision*, wherein I mentioned your letter describing how music continued in England and how you found that only natural. I did not give your name in order to make the article not too personal but everybody with some knowledge of English musical life knew that it was you. I asked the Editor to send you the article by Clipper I think you will be pleased by it. – I have not yet made definite plans but as one must assume the war to continue at least until autumn I think I shall go again to California about end of May to stay there during the summer. Next season I shall go back to the Metropolitan Opera and also take part in the 100th anniversary of New York Philharmonic as one of its guest conductors. And in spring 1942: Dear friend I hope with all my heart that then the world will have been cleaned of this pest of Nazism and Fascism, that the sunrise over a better world has begun. Now I am looking forward to return to England to see you and other dear friends again and perhaps to come back to good old Queenshall – how shall one only bear to see London again after all it had to go through to speak with all of you who had to carry the burden of these tragic happenings? I hope these lines will find you and your dear family in good health and particularly you making music 'as usual'.

Warmest greetings dear Adrian to all of you
always yours
Bruno

1709 Chevy Chase Dr. Beverly Hills California
June 15th, 41

My dear Adrian:
    This letter will be delivered to you by Erika Mann, a young friend of ours.
    She is the daughter of the famous author and poet Thomas

Mann and herself a writer of great talent and originality. But more than that she is an ardent fighter for the cause of humanity and since long has chosen to be a 'soldier' in Britain's fight. Her lecturing tours in this country and her books have procured her a great distinction.

She has spent some months of last year in England and is now going back to serve her cause again there. You will find this new 'Jeanne d'Arc' (this time fighting *for* Britain) donated with charms usually not expected with fighting natures. For not the 'Fates' or the 'Furies' but the 'Graces' befriended her in her father's house in Munich where Thomas Mann was my neighbor and our children grew up together. And so you will find her a lover of music, literature and art and just by her love of the very values of life the enemy of the Nazi-threat against humanity and culture. Added that Erika Mann has a very strong and outspoken sense of humour I think the sketch may suffice to introduce to you this young friend as a welcome occasional visitor and as an understanding listener to your music.

I thank you so much, my dear friend, for your last letter. Again it shows you going your musician's way and taking care of the cause of music unperturbed by the holocaust growing ever in extension and intensity. It seems to me that I, despite my very intense musical activity, am far more succumbing to the anxieties and hopes of the happenings and feel far more perturbed by the tragic realities of these days. I am so deeply conscious of their metaphysical meaning and I do not doubt one second that the Nazi-thrust is the strongest attack that evil has ever made in this world and that the future of mankind will be decided by the outcome of the struggle. Neither music nor any other blessing of human life could have a place or base in a Nazi-world – and so I am in every moment engaged with thought and feeling in the development of the situation. But, so far, I do not think that this passionate participation of mine has interfered with my concentration on music in my actual achievements.

Write again, dear Adrian, and continue to let me hear from time to time about your own activity and general music-life in dear old England. Let me also know if I can or shall do something in your interest in this country. I should only be too glad to do it.

> Warmest greetings to you and your family
> always yours,
> Bruno Walter.

Another voice from America was that of Arturo Toscanini. Toscanini had conducted the B.B.C. Symphony Orchestra as guest for several Festivals in pre-war days. When Boult sent him a parcel of B.B.C. war-time programmes, this telegram came back:

1st November 1941.
Thanks for programs   Your greetings and love which I reciprocate moved me to tears   I remember every one of you dear friends   I follow you with love sympathy admiration
I would like to be with you to work and share everything with you   I embrace you all   Sursum corda and we will win

> Arturo Toscanini

Later in the month came the première of Vaughan Williams's *England, my England*.

The White Gates, Westcott Road, Dorking.
13 Nov 41

Dear Adrian
I see in the *R. Times* that you are doing my England on Sunday. It may be too late when you receive this – but please remember that I have never heard it – there may be lots of miscalculations in the orchestra. Do not hesitate to modify or alter where necessary

> Yrs
> RVW

But the performance, in a programme including the *London Symphony*, disappointed Vaughan Williams.

The White Gates, Dorking
[no date]

Dear Adrian
Many thanks for your letter. We are too old and good

friends to be afraid to be honest with each other & I cannot pretend that I was not rather dismayed by the performance – As a matter of fact the 1st verse was the best – the controllers toned down the orchestra so much that it did not matter – But this was fatal in the 2nd & 3rd verses where the descant & harmonies swamped the tune – & the whole thing was sung without conviction as if they did not know it (which according to your account they do not) – Do you not think that the B.B.C. with all its tradition would have done better to cut it out altogether rather than give an unrehearsed performance? I was particularly sorry because the tune is rather a ewe lamb of mine & I feel that if it got a proper send off it might hit the nail on the head – But I felt on Sunday night that it had been strangled at birth. However several people have told me that they liked it – so perhaps I was wrong

> Yrs
> R Vaughan Wms

P.S. I did not listen to L[ondon] S[ymphony] – it evoked the past too painfully 'nessun maggiore dolore' etc – But I heard the last 8 bars which sounded very beautiful – thank you all

Then there was another letter from Bruno Walter.

1709 Chevy Chase Drive Beverly Hills California
7.6.1942

Dear Adrian!

I feel ashamed of having not written so long time. There are several reasons for this, none of them sufficient as I *very* well know: the strongest is, that one feels discouraged to write by the duration of the letter's voyage – all one can tell and says belongs to the past when the letter arrives, for the developments and events have assumed the tempo of a hurricane, their accelerando matches the rallentando of our communications by mail. Another reason is the 'bottleneck', the damming-up in our means of expression: the more overwhelmed we are by the daily happenings, the more we emotionally participate in the apocalyptic events, the less we feel able and therefore inclined to speak and express ourselves.

138

And least of all one can speak of matters remote from the region of that earthquake. In fact there are none. But, against these reasons, here is a letter just to tell you, my dear friend, that I think of you, of your dear wife and family – it was a joy to have received the snapshot you enclosed in your Christmas letter which I received in April – and that I think of dear great old England fighting for mankind and, as it becomes clearer every day, saving mankind. I am convinced that the terrific air-offensive that began with Rostock a week ago, hit Cologne and yesterday Emden, is the deciding event: the Germans cannot 'take' it – I always knew that her breakdown could be brought about only by carrying the war into the country itself.

I learn with passionate interest and hope how the growing fighting power and achievement in England is accompanied by very important developments in her social attitude and even structure. You who live there may be less aware of it than observers abroad just as somebody who sees himself dayly in the mirror cannot notice changes in his looks, but it seems to me that the unity of feeling and thinking that appears as prevailing in England is of so tremendous importance, contains so immense possibilities and promises, might prove such influential example, that the tragedy may reveal therefrom her sense. – I learned from your letter and from other reports what ardent musical life feeds English ears and souls despite all the implications of the war, and also herein I see a heartwarming promise for the future. – Here in this country the war has not yet brought any drastic changes in the musical life – so far. The continuation of the New York Philharmonic concerts in the next season is assured (I am taking more part in it than in the last two years) and of course the Metropolitan Opera certainly will also overcome its difficulties and go on. The greater Symphony-orchestras seem all to continue except the St. Louis Symphony – it would be the first victim; but, if this is to be the deeply deplorable case, we hope it will remain the only one. – The unlimited potentialities of this country become more and more realities and it is a breathtaking impression to watch the gigantic process of growing strength.

139

It is a deeply reassuring impression, but you know I personally do not need any reassurance I always was convinced of
the victory of our cause and even in the gloomiest days I had
no doubt. Old as I am I am looking forward with happy
anticipation to see the beginning at least of the new era, when
the right and the dignity of the individual, when justice and
peace will begin their definite reign. – Did you by any chance
read the address of Vice President Wallace of the U.S.A. on
the peace aims? It was the first official speech here (as far as I
know) on these questions, as lofty as 'realistic' and, as he
certainly spoke also for Roosevelt, it is the *program*, and one
with which we all can heartily agree. I hope this letter will find
you and your dear family in the best of health – warmest
greetings and wishes to all of you, also from my wife
yours in friendship
Bruno Walter

In September a programme of Beethoven and Schumann piano
concertos inspired a special tribute from Myra Hess.

48, Wildwood Road, N.W.11.
September 22nd 1942

My very dear Adrian

How can I thank you for Sunday's concert? It was entirely
due to you that the miracle happened & everyone was so
impressed by your performances with the orchestra.

I have had many touching tributes for the concertos – all my
friends say that they have never enjoyed them so much; this
from many strangers too –

I was deeply moved by the whole spirit of the concert &
your complete sympathy enabled me to concentrate entirely
on the music itself – a rare experience in concerto playing!

You said that they had gone better than ever before – so
please realise that I owe you a very great debt of gratitude –

It was one of the happiest days in my long career & I only
wish that both our beloved Mothers could have been with us –

Bless you a thousand times
Yours devotedly
Myra

P.S. Elena Gerhardt 'phoned me on Sunday evening as she was still quite excited with enthusiasm – your ears must have burned!

A few months later there was another piano concerto revival – this time for the very attenuated recording schedules of 'His Master's Voice'. It was the Concerto of Arthur Bliss which Boult and Solomon had taken to the New York World's Fair in 1939. Solomon was the soloist again for the recording, and afterwards wrote:

120, Kensington Church Street, London, W.8.
20.i.43

My dear Sir Adrian –
I *can't* tell you how much I appreciated your letter, and how much I was touched by it. It did me a power of good as I was feeling terribly tired on my return to London from Catterick – and acted as a perfect tonic!

The recording was certainly very hard work indeed – and I know that your untiring support and help made it possible for me to continue for so many hours and endeavour to keep a reasonable standard of performance.

My most grateful thanks for your truly marvellous co-operation –
                                        Yours
                                        Solomon.

Bruno Walter's latest letter, written before Christmas 1942, marvelled at the vigorous musical life in war-time of which Boult was at the centre. But he felt unable to accept the invitation to return to war-time England as John Barbirolli had recently done.

930 Fifth Avenue, New York, N.Y.
December 12th, 1942

My dear Adrian:
I feel conscience-stricken to have not yet answered your very enjoyable letter. Indeed, I was delighted to learn about all your work and endeavors and to feel the strong heartbeat of the English musical life through all the interesting details of your letter.

In fact, when the other day I had to speak at a luncheon of

141

the Metropolitan Opera League I chose as my theme the necessity of carrying on with our musical and operatic work as 'essential for the war effort'. I tried to make it clear that the home front is the moral supply base for the fighting front and, therefore, must make use of all spiritual resources, and I mentioned your description of the musical life in England which seems to be livelier than ever.

In this country we always have to speak about the importance of music in times like these because there is a certain current of opinion which wants to limit the idea of 'essential for the war effort' to a very narrow area.

So far only one of the major orchestras has disappeared, the Detroit Symphony, but you can imagine how dangerous a symptom this was and that we have to do everything in our power to prevent similar events.

The New York musical life is as strong as ever. Last season I had the satisfaction to perform Mozart's *Magic Flute* in an excellent English translation and with a very splendid success.

I am just preparing a revival of the *Marriage of Figaro* (in Italian, of course) and I am going to perform Verdi's *La Forza del Destino* in January.

My activity with the New York Philharmonic has found a better form this season as I am doing three times 2 weeks with sufficient margin in between. In former years I conducted longer times in succession and felt terribly overworked by this accumulation of concerts.

My dear Adrian, you cannot imagine how your suggestion to follow Barbirolli's example and come to England lives in my mind. Nothing could be more thrilling for me but there is a 'but'; it is the voyage. You know how unsafe still the trip on the water is and that I think my wife would simply not survive the time until my cable would tell her about my safe arrival.

Flying as the example of Barbirolli shows is reserved for journeys in direct connection with the war, and besides since my accident in Greece – do you know that my plane was hit by lightning and that I had the narrowest escape possible – I feel not yet able to fly again. Anyhow my first concert outside this

142

country will be in London and it will be one of the happiest moments in my life.

All good wishes to you, my dear friend, and to your dear family, also from my wife. And give my warmest greetings to your orchestra and all friends who still remember me.

Always affectionately yours,
Bruno

That summer Vaughan Williams's Fifth Symphony appeared with a dedication to Jean Sibelius.

The British Broadcasting Corporation
Broadcasting House, London, W.1
Box No. 7, G.P.O., Bedford.
February 14th 1944

Dear Ralph

I happened to be writing to Sibelius and without your permission I sent him the wording of your dedication. It was all done through Kurt Atterberg in Stockholm, and here is a copy of Sibelius's answer, which has just come through the same channel.

'Järvenpää, 5th January 1944

Kurt Atterberg, Esq.,
Stockholm.

Dear Atterberg,

Please accept my sincere thanks for your kind letter of the 29th December, and for your good wishes for the New Year. I wish you too a happy and prosperous New Year.

What Sir Adrian Boult and you said about my Fifth Symphony has been a source of profound pleasure to me, and I echo Sir Adrian's words about the year 1944 with all my heart.

I heard Dr. Ralph Vaughan Williams' new Symphony from Stockholm under the excellent leadership of Malcolm Sargent. This Symphony is a marvellous work. Everything in it is alive – to use the poet's words. I learnt from our newspapers of the dedication, which made me feel proud and deeply grateful. I wonder if Dr. Williams has any idea of the pleasure he has given me? The wording of the dedication was not printed in our newspapers, so I did not know it until you told me. I think your criticism, which was also published in a mutilated form in our papers, is true and to the point. I should be very grateful to you if you would convey cordial greetings from me to Sir Adrian Boult and through him to Dr. Vaughan Williams.

With kind regards and best wishes,
Yours gratefully and sincerely,
(Sgd.) JEAN SIBELIUS'

Do not bother to acknowledge
Yours Adrian

As the war news seemed to brighten, Boult renewed his invitation to Bruno Walter to renew his guest conducting with the B.B.C. Symphony.

965 Fifth Avenue New York, N.Y.
February 28, 1944.

My dear Adrian:

Many thanks for your kind letter of January 31st with all its interesting and good news. I believe to be an optimist myself, but I really cannot share your very optimistic expectation that everything will be over before the fall. Do you not feel it would be the safest way to think of my return to London for the spring 1945?

Well, let us wait and see. Anyhow, I am living in the happy presentiments of returning to the beloved and familiar places among which London takes the foremost part in my thoughts.

Many greetings to you and your dear family, also from my wife.

Always in friendship,
yours
Bruno

Among the continuing rich correspondence with composers about their music, the beginning of 1945 brought a letter from Arnold Bax about his *Summer Music* and *The Garden of Fand.*

White Horse Storrington Sussex
Sat. [6th January 1945]

My dear Adrian
   I am very pleased that you are to conduct the concert of my works on Wednesday   There are a few points I would like to mention
(a) In *Summer Music* when the cor anglais tune appears towards the end on the strings the continuity of the tune is inclined to become a little uncertain in spite of the fact that all the strings are playing this tune and the accompaniment is quite light – I could never understand why this should be, but it has never sounded quite safe except when the piece was played once with a double orchestra!
(b) In *Fand* just before the F# major tune there is a passage where the clarinet keeps up a persistent rippling arpeggio for many bars with harp playing above it. Will you please [ask] Sidonie [Goossens] to keep the harp-notes subservient so that attention to the clarinet passage is not disturbed.
(c) Near the end of the work where the sea overwhelms the island beginning in A♭ I think the brass should be marked down a little as the strings in their lower register are inclined to be swamped.
   I am looking forward so much to hearing these things. Again I thank you in advance for what I know will be some fine performances
   Best wishes for the New Year
                              from
                              Arnold.

   Following a performance of the *Sea Symphony* with Elsie Suddaby, Roy Henderson, and the Luton Choir, Vaughan Williams was still thinking experimentally about his score of 1910.

The White Gates   Dorking
Feb 1 [1945]

Dear Adrian
   Thank you very much for your letter
& 1st I want to say thank you for a splendid performance – the

145

chorus was magnificent & the two soloists covered themselves with glory – also the orchestra – but there there was the old trouble that when the chorus was singing I could not hear the orchestra – but of course that was in the hands of the control & had nothing to do with you.

As regards your special points – if you ever do it again do substitute *trombones* for *horns* at the beginning – but *not both*. The other place 'O Soul thou pleasest me' is more difficult – we have tried de-muting the 4th horn – now it sticks out too much. – Would you try a *single cello* muted *and pp added* to the 4th horn? I believe that would solve it – but it must *not* be played like a solo with lots of vibrato etc.

Ys
RVW

A broadcast of Bach's *St. John Passion* from war-time BBC headquarters at Bedford brought another letter from Vaughan Williams.

The White Gates
April 1 [1945]

Dear Adrian

We want to thank you very much for a fine performance of *St John* – clarity & emotion combined which one seldom gets together. I thought all the soloists with one exception which I will not specify were very good. If I may venture on one criticism I think the long wait between the numbers interferes with the continuity – Of course one wants pauses at the end of each episode [–] otherwise I feel that each number should be *attacca* – What a pity that the 1st Chorus is not up to the level of the rest – Would you consider one substituting 'O Mensch bewein' from *St Matthew* which I believe was originally the opening chorus of *St John*?

Your Narrator was splendid.

Our love to Ann.

Yrs
RVW

Kingsley Hotel, Bushmead Avenue, Bedford,
April 27th 1945

Dear Ralph

Thank you so much for your very kind letter about the *St John Passion*, which I thought I had answered a long time ago and find I haven't.

What you say about the stops is most interesting because I had fully intended to make a very short break after each Chorale and otherwise run right on. To my astonishment, however, dear old Charles Lofthouse did not and could not begin because he was coping with the pedals of his harpsichord, and, as you may have noticed, his figure is now making it impossible for him to see his pedals, and so we just had to wait; but it was a great shock to me particularly as the three or four worst holes were in quite unexpected places.

It was nice of you to write, and of course I am dying to know which soloist it was you did not like!
Yours ever
Adrian

A post-war performance of John Ireland's *These things shall be* brought a grateful letter from the composer.

14 Gunter Grove   Chelsea, S.W.10
August 25th, 1945

My dear Adrian,

No conventional words can be marshalled by me to express my feelings about your performance of my choral piece last night. I will not make the attempt. On the lips of all I met afterwards were spontaneous praise and admiration for your inspired and truly splendid presentation of what is embodied in this music. If it happens that I have been the amanuensis of this so urgent message, you have been the orator chosen to deliver it. And last night it was clear that the message, so unmistakably conveyed through your art, was not in vain. Something was erected which transcended any merely musical impression.

147

It was an occasion which I feel sure will not readily be forgotten by the majority of those present – and never, by me.

Yours ever,
John

A year later a further performance of the *Sea Symphony* was the cause of an appreciative letter going the other way – in this case from Lady Boult to Vaughan Williams. His characteristic little reply indulged a favourite diminution – that of referring to his most elaborate works as 'tunes':

The White Gates   Dorking
Sun 9 [September 1946]

Dear Ann

It was dear of you to write – Adrian understands that old tune of up & down – it is 36 years old next October!

Love from
Ralph

June 1947 would see the B.B.C. Orchestra's first post-war tour of Europe, including Paris, Brussels, Amsterdam, and Scheveningen. One of the Brussels programmes was to open with *Music for Strings* by Arthur Bliss.

22, Harcourt House, 19, Cavendish Square, W.1.
May 10th. [1947]

Dear Adrian.

Very many thanks for letting me know that you are playing *Music for Strings* in Brussels. I am delighted. As regards the last movement, by all means play the first scales slurred & not bowed, if you can get a more brilliant result & a slightly faster tempo. I see I have marked the Allegro con spirito ♩.= 126. I should think ♩. = 132 would be a good speed now, though I leave the actual pace to you.

With many thanks for the suggestion, and I hope you will have a good time.

Yours ever
Arthur.

A recording of the Elgar 'Cello Concerto with Pablo Casals produced another letter from the great musician.

Perpignan
29 Nov. 1947

Dear friend,[1]

What pleasure your affectionate words have given me! I want to assure you that I await with great impatience the day I am able to visit you again and to make music with you and your orchestra.

Fortunately the radio brings me in communication with you. That is at once a blessing and a sadness for me.

I imagine you very taken up in that busy London life. I congratulate you on the satisfactions you must draw from it and on the good you give to others.

The Elgar is truly magnificent – I cannot imagine a better orchestral direction than yours.

Tell your orchestra I long to see them again.

Yours affectionately
Pau Casals

The Henry Wood Concert Society, founded in 1946, planned to produce Mahler's *Symphony of a thousand* with professional soloists and a chorus and orchestra drawn from the Colleges, conducted by Boult. A letter came from Jessie Wood, Chairman of the Henry Wood Concert Society and herself a former singer.

63 Harley House, Regent's Park, N.W.1
December 2nd. 1947

Dear Sir Adrian,

I would like to tell you how glad I am that we are undertaking Mahler Eight, as it is surely one of the many idealistic journeys this Society *should* investigate. I know you will enjoy doing it, more so, since you have your own Orchestra. We have done our very best to get together a Cast efficient, and eminently suitable in voice 'colour', and we shall see to it that the ensemble is there when you come to take your full rehearsals. I have followed Bruno Walter's suggestion regarding the soprano parts – which voices he says, must be of the *still white* quality both for *No 8* and *No 2*. All other Mahler

---

[1] Translated from French

voice works require he says, the more Viennese light soprano – such as Desi Halban, with whom he has recorded No 4.

Should you at any time find a less usual manner of obtaining some publicity regarding February 10th., do please let me have it – For the chances are so remote now with cutting & yet more cutting of advertisements – & although you have been generous in giving the Society the Orchestra as well as your own invaluable support – the Society still has to foot a bill of some £1,600 – and I cannot see the box office will produce anything commensurate, in cash returns – although I devoutly hope a great artistic return will have been achieved.

With many thanks again,

Sincerely yours
Jessie Wood

Early in 1948 there was a letter from Sibelius.

Järvenpää
January 17, 1948.

Dear Sir Adrian,

Sincerely hoping that this letter does not be of inconvenience to you I would like you to know that my son-in-law, Mr. Jussi Jalas is coming to London in the beginning of February for a short stay in order to hear the best English orchestras and conductors. Mr. Jalas is a prominent musician of rare ability, has conducted several symphony-concerts here and abroad and is for the present attached to our National Opera in Helsinki. I would be very much obliged to you if he could have your permission to attend your concerts and rehearsals.

I take this opportunity to thank you for the great interest you have given to my music. It is always a great pleasure and joy to listen to your broadcasting of my compositions. In this connection I specially remember your performance of *Nightride and Sunrise* which I think one of the very best records done of my works.

Yours very sincerely,
Jean Sibelius

Broadcast performances of Vaughan Williams's *Partita* for double string orchestra brought a question from the composer about vibrato.

Broadcasting House, W.1.
1st June 1948

Dear Ralph,
Thanks so much for your letter.
I have had a word with Paul Beard [leader of the B.B.C. Symphony] to make quite certain. What we did was to have a good deal of it, particularly when the inner parts played all together, without vibrato. The opening and the top line carried just a very little, but if you are thinking of putting *senza vibrato* in the score this would, perhaps, make the performance a little too flat. It might be a useful guide to conductors if it were put against the inner parts occasionally.
I hope this is what you want.
Yours ever
Adrian

The White Gates, Dorking
10th June, 1948.

Dear Adrian
Thank you so much for your letter about 'Vibrato'. I have decided to put nothing into the score. If people cannot play it right by light of nature I feel that no amount of explanations will make them do it.
Yrs
RVW

Broadcasting House, W.1.
June 11th 1948

Dear Ralph,
Thanks so much for your letter. Forgive me if I put in my plea for the stupid performer. You have no idea, I expect, what it feels like to hanker for the composer's instructions when you are working out a score. Sibelius is, of course, the

151

most maddening of all, but it is the greatest comfort to have metronome marks and indications like *'vibrato'* or *'non-vibrato'* or a note about the general treatment at the beginning of the score or the beginning of the movement, so please do not expect too much from the interpreter. He may misunderstand your instructions, but that is one stage better than having none.

Yours ever
Adrian

Later in the same month Vaughan Williams wrote about the broadcasting of his new Sixth Symphony.

The White Gates, Dorking.
24th June, 1948.

Dear Adrian

Symphony in E. minor

I listened to the broadcast the other day so far as my wireless allowed, but as usual now with the Third Programme it rattled and howled and also invented a brand new noise rather like a banshee, which went on most of the time. Nevertheless I managed to hear it was a fine performance, for which I thank you.

This was the first time I heard it over the wireless and I note two points.

One is – full score Page 60 at Fig. 18: The crotchet E on the Timpani had better come out because it obscures the harmony, at all events over the wireless.

The other point is that in the Scherzo the side drum sounded over the wireless to be still muffled as it is in the slow movement. Do you think the player did not tighten his snares, or whatever he does, to get that very sharp high sound which I want? I wonder if you could ask him next time you see him what the proper direction should be to get that effect, and if there is still time I will have it put into the score.

Yrs
RVW

The aftermaths of war were still everywhere. Rudolf Schwarz

had moved straight from refugee status into conductorship of the Bournemouth Symphony Orchestra. In addition to all a conductor's regular duties, he was sitting up every night trying to absorb the entire repertory of British orchestral works. To learn all this in a thorough, traditional way was a manifest impossibility, and he appealed to Boult for advice. Boult told him of a technique learned from conducting much modern music at the Royal College of Music in the 1920's: grasp the tempo and 'the rough up and down of it' and you will get through. 'The orchestra will do things for you if you will let them. Beat the time and they'll follow you.'

Bournemouth
26/6/49

Dear Sir Adrian,

. . . Now let me especially thank you most gratefully for your inestimable advice! To tell you briefly: I did follow it, quite spontaneously, and the result really was remarkable. I went to the Rostrum, told the Orchestra I had no idea of the score (it was a manus[cript], badly written), concentrated as you said mainly on Tempo and Rhythm, and the whole thing went better than anything at any time before. I was speechless.

Then I tried it more often, especially when I found a manuscript difficult and tiresome to decipher, and the result remained the same.

I don't believe in miracles, so I tried to find an explanation. I think it is this: half measures are of no use, either a score can be studied properly and one feels safe and free, or one should tackle it as you said; provided that sight-reading as such means no problem, and the Orchestra is of some standard. (Now I also understand what you meant by saying: I should take more risks.) The advantage then is having a calm mind and a balanced disposition, approaching the work with less ambition as to details, and being less anxious about difficulties, because one does not know them at all and is not worrying all the time that they might not be overcome.

It is a strange thing, but I gained a lot of self-confidence by this experience, and I really don't know how to thank you. Of course, I agree with you, this remedy should not be recommended to everybody; whoever adopts this attitude as a general one will and must become a Charlatan. It only is *the* solution if 24 hours a day do not suffice for all the work to be done.

. . . May I once more thank you most sincerely for all your great kindness and generous help. I cannot express to you, Sir Adrian, how much encouragement I and we all have received from you.

Ever gratefully yours,
Rudolf Schwarz

It is easily forgotten that we were still living in something like *war* conditions. Food rationing still existed, and life in many ways was very uncomfortable – in fact, some of our homes were still requisitioned. For this reason I never rehearsed the orchestra for one minute longer than I thought necessary, often stopping well before the scheduled close. When this was reported to the senior B.B.C. officials responsible for finance, they were displeased. Nobody ever complained openly of unrehearsed performances (I don't think there were any), and I doubt whether it can be said that I was responsible for the fact that the B.B.C. Symphony Orchestra of 1951 was not quite the superb instrument it had been in 1939. After all it was smaller by twenty players, and many of the leaders had changed.

. . . I seem to have been working very hard for these last B.B.C. years. I knew that the B.B.C. had a dismissal rule on reaching sixty-one, and that I should come under it in April 1950. A casual remark made by one whose position was much senior to mine gave me hope of extension, and this was not uncommon at that time. However, I was given due notice to go exactly on the official date.

After twenty years' service the B.B.C.'s farewell arrangements were generous. At a small luncheon party in Broadcasting House, Sir William Haley spoke in such kind terms that I began to wonder whether I had really been asked to go or had insisted on going, to their great regret.[1]

[1] *My own trumpet*, pp. 147–9.

III. 'Fear not to sow because of the birds'
1950–1978

This was Canon Barnett's favourite quotation, placed on his tomb in Westminster Abbey in 1913. That was at the beginning of Adrian Boult's career, and it became a favourite thought of his own. In 1950, at the end of a seeming life-work in British Broadcasting, the longest phase of that career lay still before him.

As soon as this news [of B.B.C. retirement] became public property I was greatly honoured by an approach from Mr Thomas Russell, then Manager of the London Philharmonic Orchestra, and as it turned out, I was only unemployed for two or three days . . .

Thomas Russell rightly believed in frequent tours abroad. It is a great incentive to finer playing, and the freshness of approach intrigues foreign audiences, just as foreign orchestras intrigue us here. Tiring though they are, these tours stimulate morale, and there is always better playing not only on the tour, but afterwards.[1]

A German tour for January 1951 included British works and classics. One of the works was the Beethoven Seventh Symphony, and even now Boult found himself wondering about the dynamic shape of the 'Allegretto' second subject. He wrote to Dr. Hedwig Kraus at the Gesellschaft der Musikfreunde in Vienna to ask whether the composer's manuscript shed any light.

Gesellschaft der Musikfreunde in Wein
January 11th 1951

Dear Sir,
Thank you for your letter of December 19th 1950, which I

[1] *My own trumpet*, pp. 147 and 151.

155

got yesterday, It is a very interesting thing what you are asking for and I am only sorry to tell you, that the original manuscript of Beethovens 7th Symphony is not in our possession.

But I could look in the first editions not only of the parts, but also of the score (which had been edited later) and besides these editions we are possessing the piano-partition of the 7th symphony written by Anton Diabelli and corrected by Beethoven.

Therefore I am able to give you here the various kinds, in which the crescendo- and decrescendo-signs are standing in these old sources. ... I think that the signs in the early editions and the manuscript show rather clearly, that the culmination of the crescendo is in the 7th bar.

I am regretting it very much that there should not be an occasion for you to come to Vienna once more; I think you enjoyed Vienna and Austria very much when you came and conducted in our concerts.

With best greetings.

yours truly

Dr. Hedwig Kraus

Archivdirektor

On 6th May 1951 a National Festival of Schools' Music was held at the Royal Albert Hall. The Executive Committee included Bernard Shore, former principal violist of the B.B.C. Symphony Orchestra and now Inspector of Music in Schools for the Ministry of Education. He invited Boult, as President of the Schools' Music Association and the National Youth Orchestra, to conduct the concert. The programme included a Vaughan Williams Cantata, *The Sons of Light*, composed for the Festival to words especially written by the poet Ursula Wood (who was to become Vaughan Williams's second wife). It concluded with a Psalm arrangement by Holst for all forces. Boult brought the London Philharmonic Orchestra. After the interval he conducted the National Youth Orchestra in Elgar's *Cockaigne* Overture and Bizet's *L'arlesienne* suite no. 1. Afterwards came this letter from Bernard Shore.

32 Launceston Place, London, W.8
May 7 1951.

My dear Adrian
I don't think I have ever admired you more than yesterday
– and taking on that appalling task – not just of the Concert –
but all the preparations.
I am quite sincere when I say that without you, we should
never have brought this off.
I think the work itself will have tremendous repercussions,
and rather naturally, I could scarcely sit in my seat, taking
everything into consideration.
These Dear People, who have had so little really nice
experience have now had a pretty big one, and they are
really grateful. They at any rate do know what *you* mean to
them.
Do take care of yourself, and not be too much at people's
beck & call – yet I know what you feel. There are certain calls
that are important, perhaps, for the 'National' picture of
music and it was such a call yesterday. So I hope I shan't be
instrumental in worrying you again yet awhile!
I thought the way you built up all the focal points of the
whole programme – and the glorious climax in the Holst
Hymn – quite heavenly.
                    Bless you
                    Bernard

Vaughan Williams had instituted annual performances of the
Bach Passions at Dorking. At the age of 80 he still conducted them,
and for the *St. John* in March 1953 Boult was present.

The White Gates,
Dorking, Surrey.
18th March, 1953.

Dear Adrian
It was wonderful of you to come the other night, and your
praise has been a great stimulus.

157

As regards standing up to sing, of course I do not hear all the clatter and noise from where I stand and I feel, during a long session like that people like to stand up occasionally. I do not think they would join in so well if they sang sitting down, but I admit the clatter and interruption is annoying.

As regards how I do the different chorales, I am afraid I have no principles but do what I think is going to sound best. There are one or two considerations, however. I can only ask the audience to join in the ones they know well; I am gradually adding to the number, and some of the more meditative ones I feel can be sung softly unaccompanied. You mention, 'Thy will be done'. This seems to me ought to be meditative and soft, not an agonised shout like ''Tis I', and the same applies, of course, to the very soft chorale 'Be with me, Lord.'

Sometimes the effect was meant to be purely musical as when, in the chorale with two verses I have the first verse sung solo quartette and then answered by the whole body of people. Sometimes the reason is dramatic as in the chorale after 'Let Him be crucified', which obviously has to stand out as something different from the shout that has gone before it. If I had sufficient singers I would detail a small semi-chorus to sing that off-stage, but by singing with only half the choir very softly we nearly get that effect.

I hope I am gradually improving the general conception of the thing and I shall think over all your ideas very carefully.

Thank you again so much for coming. I shall tell my singers of your praise.

> My love to Ann
> Yrs fr [om] both
> Ralph

March 23rd 1953

Dear Ralph

How very kind of you to answer so fully. I am afraid I must have said something stupid because I felt that everyone of the chorales was completely and splendidly appropriate, and am quite sure that those in Part II were equally so. It was just that

158

I jibbed at the interruption even when the Choir only stood up after 'Thy Will be done'. I see no reason why some should not be sung unaccompanied.

It was a great performance and the further off it is, the greater it seems – you know what I mean!

Yours ever

Adrian

Boult's direction of the London Philharmonic Orchestra involved a heavy schedule of gramophone recordings. One of the most important of these was the first complete cycle of Vaughan Williams Symphonies ever committed to disc. On 10th and 11th December 1953 they reached the most recent, the *Antartica*. The composer was present in the studio with his wife Ursula, who during one 'take' of the Scherzo drew an impromptu cartoon.

A drawing by Ursula Vaughan Williams made during the first recording of *Sinfonia Antartica*, December 1953.

A friend of many years was Yehudi Menuhin. Correspondence went back into the 1930's, but many early letters have disappeared. The depth of the friendship was shown in 1955 in an exchange of letters after the loss of a child.

South Hawke, Woldingham, Surrey.
3 September 1955

Dear Yehudi –

Ann & I were deeply shocked to get your letter & its sad sad news – at such times it is only a deep faith that can sustain you, &, as you wisely say, the hope that time will gradually help to make the awful gap a little bit smaller. I suppose we shall someday be allowed to know why such dreadful things can happen: there must be a reason but it is impossible to see it from this earthly life. Ann will be writing to Diana – she suffered an almost identical loss many years ago, & recently we have lost a grandchild 17 months old.

In another letter you spoke very kindly of coming to London to play with another orchestra. This is as it should be: the LPO & I value enormously the privilege of playing with you – more than with *anyone* else – but we must not expect a monopoly: that would be wrong!

Much love to you both from us both, & every good wish to you all for an unclouded future –

Yrs always
Adrian.

19750 Alma Bridge Road, Los Gates, California
September 20, 1955

Dear Adrian:

I read Diana your sweet letter and she was very moved. She also felt deeply for the grandchild and for the mother.

160

One cannot help always returning to the great question 'why?'. That is where every living thing encounters the ultimate mystery. We only have within a limited degree a certain measure of control over our lives and I am convinced that we are expected within that scope to exercise our will and our intelligence and all the qualities which one tries to apply to one's existence, but all of them, even when exercised to the full can still not bring control or completely change Fate. After all, the individual life is not only held accountable for its own existence and behaviour but for all that preceded it. In other words, for the existence and behaviour of countless generations preceding it, and of its own family, nation, and complete universal environment; a completely innocent individual, and how many millions have there been within our own lifetime who have paid with their lives for the stupidity and vanity of statesmen, chemists, doctors, parents, etc. There is nothing more depressing than innocence wronged. However, for my part, this is additional proof that we cannot consider ourselves as isolated units in creation, for being held accountable for debts beyond our immediate control should prove that we cannot really consider ourselves innocent of guilt so long as we are part and parcel of a larger ignorance or a larger intelligence.

Diana is looking forward to receiving a letter from Ann.

I am playing on April 8th, as I wrote, with another orchestra and even with another conductor! This is, however, not 'as it should be', as you write. It is merely so because apparently you are not free on that date, which is unfortunately the one Sunday I am in England between January and September or October.

Our love to you both,
Yehudi

A year later came a Menuhin biography by Robert Magidoff, written with the full assistance of the subject. A copy promptly arrived inscribed 'To dear Adrian from your old friend Yehudi, London, Oct. 1956.'

53 Welbeck Street, London, W.1
6 November 1956

My dear Yehudi –

Your book, & its lovely dedication, came several weeks ago, but I have only just finished it – reading time has been so restricted. It is putting it much too low to say that I have been fascinated. As a human document it is, if I may say so, wonderfully charming & exceedingly well written. But it is far *more* notable, I think, for the way in which you have released the intimate technical side of your life. It will surely be of *immense* value to those students who have the sense to learn from it, & the account of your first talk with Diana is a revelation which is a landmark in the history of teaching – I mean teaching with a capital T, not just music teaching. The teaching world owes you an immense debt which I hope it will have the sense to recognise. To me, whose development has been fatally easy (I might have been a better artist if it had been more difficult) it has itself been a great lesson, for which I am profoundly grateful.

I was so sick, that when someone with authority came back to the Decca office, they said they *would* have allowed me to do the Bruch. I *was* a fool not to have found it out before they went away. Well, I hear there are some nice dates ahead for us!

No answer to all this – I look forward to our meeting

Love to you all

Yrs always
Adrian.

In 1956 Vaughan Williams, at the age of 84, founded the R.V.W. Trust. His wife Ursula recalled:

One of the things Ralph had long wanted was to give a concert of Gustav [Holst]'s lesser-known works. When the plans for the Trust were well advanced he had discussed this with Adrian, and the Festival Hall had been booked and the programme chosen.

162

10, Hanover Terrace, Regents Park, London, N.W.1.

My dear Adrian,

I think your idea of changing the order of the programme for the Holst Concert, and putting *The Morning of the Year* second, and the Choral Fantasia directly after the interval is a good one.

I saw Imogen [Holst] yesterday and she is delighted and excited, and tells me that her mother is also coming to the concert.

Our love to you both,

Yrs
Ralph

Programme notes for the concert on 10th December were written by Scott Goddard, Herbert Howells, and Edmund Rubbra. Afterwards Boult and his wife wrote separate letters of appreciation to Vaughan Williams, who replied:

10, Hanover Terrace, Regents Park, London, N.W.1.
December 13th 1956.

Dear Ann and Adrian,

Thank you both for your wonderful letters. Adrian, you did wonders, and Ann, it was everything having you there.

I hear that there were a lot of young people there who were much excited over the music.

All love from us
Ralph

One of the casualties of World War II had been Michael Heming, killed in action at El Alamein in 1942 at the age of 22. The son of the baritone Percy Heming and his wife Joyce, Michael had not yet decided between conducting – to which his love of Elgar's music especially drew him – and composing. Some fragmentary sketches had been completed by Anthony Collins as a *Threnody for a soldier killed in action*. Boult had known Percy Heming for years before that. In the autumn of 1957 he planned another performance of Michael's *Threnody* with the LPO in Bristol. Mrs. Heming sent her son's copy of Elgar's Second Symphony in gratitude.

31E, Abbey Road, St. John's Wood, N.W.8.
22.10.57

My dear Adrian.

. . . You may wonder at the enclosed score – Dear Adrian, if you will, I want you to please accept it. It was, of course, Micky's. I think it was his favourite Symphony & he took this score with him to Egypt & it was one of the few things he took up into the desert with him, & it came back to us – I cherish it very much, & for that reason, & while I am still here, I want you to have it – You have been so good & generous to me – I shall never forget it, or for your help over the *Threnody*. The rest of Micky's music will go to young Alastair Kisch but he has no affinity with Elgar, & anyway I have set my heart on your having it. There are little indications of the mental pictures that the music conjured up in Micky's mind, as on page 159 – 'The level lake & the long glories of the Winter moon'. Perhaps, sometime, if you want to run through the score in a train or somewhere, it may be useful. I feel so happy for you to have it, for you can have no idea how I cherish my friendship with you & dear Ann, or how grateful I am to you both for all you have done for me –

My love to you both,
Yours
Joyce.

Time was passing. Boult decided he must give up Musical Directorship of the LPO. The association continued in concerts and recordings. In August 1958 they were to record Vaughan Williams's last Symphony in the presence of the composer, but in the night the old man died, and the recording became a memorial. In April 1959 came Boult's 70th birthday, and among the flood of telegrams and letters came one from Sir Robert Mayer, who had founded the Children's Concerts with Boult as conductor almost forty years earlier.

Hotel Lotti, Paris.
2/IV/59.

My dear Adrian,

So you will be three-score-&-ten in a few days. When the

sages of my race envisaged 70 years as the *comble* in a man's life they could not envisage the negation of this theory by men like yourself who are easily jumping over this milestone & continuing their activities with undiminished vigour & enthusiasm. But then you were fortunate enough to have chosen a profession which is also your great love & inspiration.

May Dorothy and I join the chorus of your friends and well-wishers in wishing you very many more years of health and happiness.

Yours ever
Robert M.

The B.B.C. planned a memorial to Vaughan Williams in the form of two broadcasts of *The Pilgrim's Progress* with Boult conducting the Orchestra and Chorus from whose Directorship he had retired almost ten years earlier. He consulted Ursula Vaughan Williams about metronome markings.

10, Hanover Terrace, Regents Park, London, N.W.1.
July 6th 1959

My dear Adrian,

The metronome was long after the *Pilgrim*, and I should be *much* more inclined to trust your own understanding of what Ralph wanted – you have always been so close to his thinking. The only thing I can say with *absolute* certainty about this work is that he set greatest store of all by people being able to 'sing a tune'. I know the leaves of life ladies had to be bullied & bullied, & he never got quite the phrasing & flow he wanted. But this was a particular application of a *passionate* general principle. Dennis Arundell is coming on the 14th. I want to talk Appolyon to him in *case* we ever get to the Edinburgh stage – I hope you will still be away for your sakes, but if you *are* secretly in London, & were free at 6 how nice it would be.

I'm going to Italy, to swelter on the Golfo di Paradiso, from July 27th – that is, train to Lyons, & then 2 days in Provence, which I know a little, & love, the rest of the party don't know, & then just plain seaside, no sightseeing – I am taking 3 swim suits & trust to be entirely amphibious.

I've lent Leonard Isaacs the record of the Passion – record companies having failed so far – & hope there *may* be a chance of a broadcast – & I live in a curious mixture of watering the garden & a new, huge, terrible filing cabinet.

Imogen & I have just finished our index for the letters [between Holst and Vaughan Williams] & are off to the O[xford] U[niversity] P[ress] to discuss bindings – I suppose it'll be delayed now, though.

Love to you both, & do enjoy your holiday
         Ursula.

After the recordings for broadcast in December, Mrs. Vaughan Williams wrote again.

10, Hanover Terrace, Regents Park, London, N.W.1.
December 7th 1959

My dear Adrian

I cannot thank you enough for the most lovely *Pilgrim*. The whole performance had a unity and strength and serenity which was completely satisfying – & shattering, both together.

Michael Kennedy asked me to tell you how completely desolated he was at not being there; his Editor was whipped off to hospital on Thursday & he has had to take charge. As Steuart was here for the Composers' Guild luncheon & was terribly anxious to hear the *Pilgrim* again – I gave him the Kennedys' passes: as it was Saturday – & too late to get new ones from Mrs Beckett – like all the rest of our friends he was full of admiration. I expect your telephone has not ceased ringing – like mine – with loving & grateful listeners wanting to say thank you. The orchestra were (?was) glowing, & I see more & more how brilliantly Ralph used instruments for characters & characterization. I have learned so much from being allowed to come to rehearsals, and I am particularly grateful – rehearsals have been so much of my life for the last twenty years I couldn't bear not to be involved in what go on being new creative moments with Ralph's work.

My love to you both, & great gratitude to Ann for her

elegant picnics, surely only Marie Antionette ever had such picnics before!

Ursula.

Early in 1960 Boult was asked to be guest on 'Desert Island Discs'. One of his choices was Brahms's *Der Schmied*, recorded early in the century by Elena Gerhardt with Nikisch at the piano. He wrote to Elena Gerhardt to ascertain the playing speed of the old record.

53, Redington Road, Heath Drive, London, N.W.3.
March 13th 1960.

My dear Adrian –
Many thanks for your very kind letter. I am very touched that you want to take my record 'Der Schmied' with Nikisch's accompaniment with you to the 'Desert Island'. I sang it actually in H dur [i.e., B major] – as by the time I made it I was not so 'original Key' conscious – as I became later. Luckily I had quite a big range for a Mezzo – and got easily up to B flat – which enabled me to sing almost every Lied in the original Key.

I listen most interested to your talks on Conducting – naturally – because *we* were brought up in it. Richard Strauss often emptied his heart out to me – about other Conductors – saying that I seemed to be 'ein halbes Conductor myself'. Of course this sounds funnier in his Bavarian dialekt.

I shall listen in on the 28th of course – and thanking you very much again for putting this record in

With warmest greetings
Yours always
Elena Gerhardt.

After the broadcast she wrote again.

53, Redington Road, Heath Drive, London, N.W.3.
March 30th 1960.

Dear Adrian
your Desert Island was most interesting and for me very moving. The end of the *Oberon* – Ouverture – conducted by

Nikisch brought old and wonderful times most vividly back to me. I was touched by your devotion to him.

I felt very honored to be included in such an illustrious Company of Musicians – and very grateful to you for such a happy half hour.

I wonder if you have any Manuscript of Nikisch's writing Music? He orchestrated some Songs for me – when I sang Concerts with Orchestra accompaniments – and in gratitude I hope you will accept the enclosed Manuscript of his Orchestration of Beethoven – Goethe's *Die Ehre Gottes*.

With many thanks again and warmest greetings
Elena.

In December Boult conducted a performance of the Beethoven Violin Concerto for Yehudi Menuhin – who had appeared earlier at the Royal College of Music at the invitation of its new director, Keith Falkner. After the Beethoven concert, Boult wrote this letter:

93 Whitehall Ct., S.W.1.
10 December 1960.

My dear Yehudi.

I seem to have a lot to say to you, & so please forgive all this when you are thinking of weddings &, I hope, great happiness. There is nothing urgent at all, & I don't expect an answer!

I hope you enjoyed your time at the RCM. I hear lyrical accounts of it all. Keith Falkner & I are old friends.

Sunday was, as always with you, a wonderful experience. Have you ever played the Beethoven more splendidly? Perhaps in the first movement when I somehow felt I was not really with you, & that *must* have affected you, though I hope not, – certainly didn't hear anything: I just felt that I hadn't taken your spirit as an accompanist should. But after that it was wonderful I felt, & hope it *all* was for you.

And now I want to ask you to think over one small point about the cadenzas. Are they getting too fast? Your fabulous technique is of course fully equal to it all, but I did feel particularly where the two themes come together it could

168

have sounded still more noble, if it had been a little broader –
I wonder?

By the bye, did you hear that the apparently good-natured
suggestion that we should rehearse on Sunday afternoon
involved *5 hours* with Dorati on Sunday morning, then *us*;
afternoon & evening. What *would* the poor orchestra have
been like after all that?

Every good wish to you both from us both, & specially to
your young people.

> Yrs always
> Adrian

The year 1961 opened with a very charming tribute from
the London Philharmonic Orchestra to the man who had
begun to be their permanent conductor ten years before. It
was a delightful idea to commemorate our ten years' work
together, and to persuade Yehudi Menuhin to play the Elgar
Violin Concerto at the concert. When the time came he was
unable to play. . . .[1]

Randolph Hotel, Oxford
23 December 1960

My dear Yehudi.

I was just thinking of answering your lovely long letter,
when the awful news broke upon us. However today's paper
gives it as slight, & only a month's postponement of dates, so
Ann & I feel comforted, & I'm sure poor Diana must feel
better though one can never be happy until these things are
safely over. And we hope yours soon will be.

Greenhouse Allt tells me that there is just a chance we may
have the luck of your cooperation at the Royal Concert next
November. That would be wonderful, & will be some conso-
lation for this present disappointment.

You write very generously of the Beethoven, but I'm sure it
was my fault – working with you is always such a thrill, one is
particularly keen to try for perfection.

[1] *My own trumpet*, p. 167.

When we meet I want to ask you to tell me of the last recordings you have made. We played the Beethoven the other day – I have never heard your record of the Brahms: are you happy about that? And I have never received a copy of the Sibelius we so enjoyed with you, so I suppose it hasn't been issued yet?

Ann (who sends love & every good wish) & I are here for the week where 6 grandchildren collect (5 miles away) with much noise & excitement we expect. They range from 10 to 1 so there is plenty of variety!

When we get back we are going straight to see *Emil* [a play with Menuhin's son Gerard]. I do hope you will be able to see it. It will be great fun – I hope he is enjoying it all! Those first flights *are* fun. Poor Diana will be torn in half between the Clinic & the theatre.

Well – we look forward to seeing lots of good reports about you, & a very quick recovery. We join in every good wish for a good New Year & lots of HEALTH.

Yrs always
Adrian

9th January, 1961.

Dear Adrian,

I feel so unhappy that I shall not share in the tribute to you on January 17th. It is an occasion which, as you must know, and must feel, is very close to my heart, as for so many years we have shared the London public, the violin concertos of Beethoven, Brahms, Bartok. We have lived many wonderful moments together, and ever since, as a child, or rather as a young man, I first came under your benign baton, I have always treasured this association. Now, on the very occasion when these feelings could be expressed, both in music and in words, I am denied the opportunity.

Although I could come to the concert, and at least make an appearance carrying a laurel wreath to lay on your head at the interval, I am wondering whether it is advisable for me, vis-à-vis the public, to be seen on the very occasion when I should have played, without my violin – do you think they might say 'Well if he is well enough to walk and talk he must obviously be well enough to play the violin'. Do you think it is advisable in view of this possible reaction for me to come to the concert? I would so love to.

Regarding your sweet letter, I am not happy about my last Beethoven concerto recording at all, and as for the Brahms, I know I can play it much better, and the same applies to a great many records, in fact the majority, which I never listen to once the recording is made! However, there is always the hope and the aim, which must remain a little bit above one-self, and to that extent it is a healthy attitude. Perhaps there will be a few records which will survive the test of time. I feel I have just made some very good recordings of the Paganini concertos, wherein at least three notes are ideal, and of the *Poème* of Chausson, which I did as a tribute to Georges Enesco, for it is the one piece that I feel I imbibed by osmosis almost bodily from him, as well as some recordings of the Beethoven Romances, and some movements of the Bach Suites for orchestra, which I think may be creditable.

It was so good of you to go to see Gerard in his play *Emil*, so characteristic of your thoughtfulness towards the young and your encouragement of their efforts. He is having great fun, very proud and very happy.

Meanwhile I am making excellent progress and am sure that within the month, or at least by the beginning of February, I shall be back in harness again.

Diana joins in our love to you and Ann,
Always your devoted
Yehudi

But Menuhin managed to be present at the commemoration concert on 17th January 1961.

He . . . was well enough to come to the Hall and present to me a beautifully bound copy of the Bliss 'Colour Symphony' (probably the first work that had honoured me with its dedication), signed by the composer and everyone in the L.P.O. Campoli played the Elgar very finely in Menuhin's place, and we also played a Dance Concerto 'Phalaphala' by Priaulx

Rainier which had been specially written for the concert.[1]

Absent friends also sent tributes. One was Nadia Boulanger.

Écoles d'Art Américaines,
Palais de Fontainebleau
Jan 17th 1961

Dear Sir Adrian,
This evening 'concert is a tribute to Adrian Boult' How could I not join all those who love & admire you – And here I am, clapping hands, heart beating to celebrate the one to whom we owe so much
Feel all what these awkward, hasty lines bring you in deep respect for the man, the conductor, the musician, the artist & believe in my devoted friendship so proud of yours, my dear Friend
                    Nadia Boulanger

A few weeks later came a letter from another distinguished international musician, the composer Paul Hindemith. It was a friendship of a quarter-century, as Boult himself recalled.

Hindemith had visited the B.B.C. several times after 1930, and in 1936 he arrived on the night of the death of King George V. Hindemith was to play the Walton Viola Concerto in Queen's Hall for a broadcast the next day, but we felt this would not be appropriate for what must become a memorial concert. After we had discussed all possible works that he could play, and dismissed them all, our guest delighted us by offering to compose something. We loaded him with music paper and in a few hours the beautiful *Trauermusik* for viola and strings was ready. It made a deep impression.

Some years later, in the autumn of 1939, the B.B.C. received a puzzled letter from the authorities at Gibraltar to say that a German called Hindemith had been intercepted on his way from Turkey (the Turkish government had given him a commission to reorganise their music) to the United States,

[1] *My own trumpet*, p. 167.

and quoted the B.B.C. as vouching for the importance of his further passage to America. I wrote a pompous letter on B.B.C. notepaper recommending his further journey and assuring that he was a man of peace.

When he visited London in 1961 I had to be away, so I wrote to send him good wishes . . .

Vevey, poste restante
March 6th, 1961.

Dear Sir Adrian:

Your most touching letter conjured up quite a number of cherished memories and I thought it might give you a particular satisfaction to have the original sketch of 'our' Music of mourning which I wrote in one of the B.B.C.'s dungeons in January 1936 the day after His Majesty died. I remember very clearly our playing of the piece the same night, and how doleful we all were, many of the musicians weeping. I don't remember having a regular score of the piece, as I had just enough time to copy the parts. I think I had compiled a kind of particelle, from which you conducted – this and the parts have probably disappeared in the archives of the B.B.C. So if you care for this memory-burdened piece at all (as I do and always did, in spite of its pettiness) this is all I can send you. But if on the other hand you prefer to have something more representative, beautifully copied and worked out rather calligraphically – as this old fussy writer usually does – I trust you will let me know what kind of score you would like to have instead of (or together with) this rather shabby-looking bit of music.

It was a pity that we had no opportunity of discussing these things orally when we were in London, but I hope there will be a way of making up for this defect another time.

I am, with best regards to you and Mrs. Boult, from both of us

Yours
Paul Hindemith

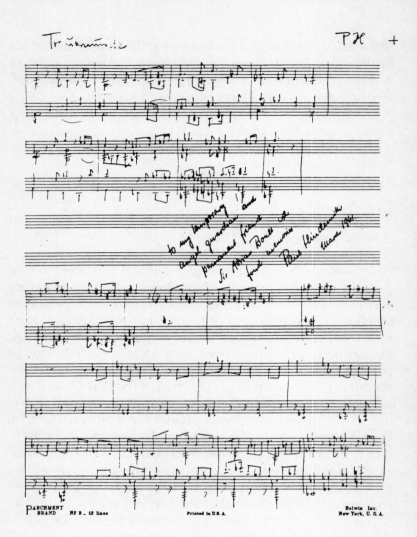

Then came a letter from the United States practically surveying the development of music during these later years of Boult's lengthening career. The writer was Dr. John Vincent, himself a composer and the Boults' host during a visit to California seven years earlier.

Huntington Hartford Foundation, Pacific Palisades,
California
April 9, 1961

Dear Adrian,
   Our annual festival is just about all set now although it has
been a terrible struggle. There have been grave financial
obstacles and this has had personality under- and over-tones.
Fortunately, most of these difficulties are overcome and,
although we are very late, the complete programs will be
released in a day or so.
   Iain Hamilton will be the English composer represented. I
hope you think the choice a good one. Since this festival is
mainly limited to composer-conductors, the field of choice
was very narrow. We would have liked to have had Walton or
Britten but they were unavailable. I thank you for your help
and suggestions.
   Your remarks about the prevalence of twelve-tone advo-
cates among the younger composers is [sic] interesting: I had
not had confirmation of this in England before. Personally,
while I believe that it is not impossible to write worth-while
music in this idiom, the present emphasis on it seems to me to
be artificial and unfortunate. And it cannot be said to be new
or experimental: it is really 'old hat' and a follow-the-leader
kind of conformity. Under the pretext of being 'modern', a lot
of young men are fooling no one so much as themselves.
   A curious commentary is that here in California, where
Schoenberg taught eight years ago at UCLA, the wave of
12-tone music seems to be receding. As you probably know, I
was the next teacher of composition at UCLA after Schoenberg and so I have had a good vantage point to see the
progress of the movement. During the first years (the early
'50s and the late '40s), there were some very militant tone-
row composers in my class. Later they were less violently
disposed but this is the first year that I have not a single
twelve-toner! And, up and down the coast, there are very few
practitioners – despite Stravinsky's late capitulation to the
technique.

There are still a lot of twelve-tone and serial composers in and around New York – and quite a group of electronic ones (if they can be called composers). (As an aside, it was interesting to me to attend a hearing of the electronic music from Japan while in New York last week: the audience was small, unenthusiastic and, bored beyond endurance, either drifted out before the end or began talking very openly! This is the music of the future! If I thought so I would be a lot more reconciled to the extinction which some anticipate.) Europe and Japan seem to be the chief strong-holds of twelve-tone technique. It is thus that the incidence of Schoenberg's influence increases with the square of the distance from Los Angeles, where he lived his last 16 years! This is a law worthy of some Teutonic label like 'die Rückwirkungrück'.

> . . . Sincerely yours,
> John

Then came a final greeting from Bruno Walter, also in California – full of old friendship but sadly dispirited at the turns music had taken at the end of his life.

608 North Bedford Drive, Beverly Hills, California
May 14th 1961

My dear Adrian!

You 'wondered if I would care to read what you wrote after reading my book' – let me tell you that nothing, really nothing could have made me happier, could give me higher satisfaction than such words of consent from a musician of your stature. It was my hope to receive such a 'nod' from a distinguished colleague like you as a response to my musical confessions in an epoch, when the whole edifice of our musical culture is tottering on its foundations; in other words: when we experience an invasion of musical atheism in our sanctuaries. Thank you, my dear friend, for having received my confessions with open arms, for having supported them with the weight of your authority. – How I wished I could come once more to London, to see you and the beloved city again and renew old ties! – But very soon I shall be 85 years old and, although in relatively good health, I do not think I should undertake long trips – I also have given up public appearances – my conducting activity is limited to making records – but I go on learning, reading, studying and occasionally writing.

I hope you and your family in good health and in good mood – as good as the evil spirits who seem to dominate our contemporary history will permit.

Thanking you once more of all my heart and with my warmest wishes your old friend

Bruno

Yet Boult himself retained his interest in the music of his time. In 1961 he appeared with his old orchestra, the B.B.C. Symphony, during the Prom season:

Another very pleasant compliment was paid me that year by Malcolm Williamson, who had been commissioned by the B.B.C. to write a work for the Henry Wood Promenades. It took the form of an organ concerto, played by the composer, each movement of which was built on one of my initials A.C.B.[1]

The premiere took place on 8th September, and after it came a letter from the young composer-soloist.

2, Lyndhurst Gardens, N.W.3.
13.ix.61

Dear Sir Adrian,

Your very kind letter overwhelmed me. I wish I thought that my piece was more worthy of its dedication. I have heard the recording taken from the radio and it is good. As far as the orchestra goes it is excellent. Your tempi, phrasing and balance all admirable. The organ playing could have been better and more precise. I do hope we can do it again. I was very touched by the gift of the chocolates with Lady Boult's note. Please thank her for me.

It was a curious and humbling feeling to play under your direction. There is a hypnotism which you spread over the

[1] *My own trumpet*, p. 167.

orchestra which elevates every player, and which moved & inspired me greatly. I am sure there is nobody to compare with you technically and spiritually except Bruno Walter; I couldn't believe my slow movement was capable of such marvellous life!

I felt badly battered by criticism, but some of it was good, and I have had congratulatory messages from [Ralph] Downes, [organist at the Brompton Oratory and designer of the Royal Festival Hall organ], [Alan] Wicks [organist of Canterbury Cathedral], & Dr. Steinitz amongst others. Yesterday I received a very hurtful anonymous letter in the same mail as Dr. Steinitz's praising one; and last night a stream of vituperation from a man in Bromley, Leeds, which is not without its funny side. I quote – 'Sir A. Boult must have felt a right Charlie at having this muck thrust onto him.' I guess my correspondent visualised you sight-reading the score at the performance.

As I tried to say on the 'phone, your Prom season was a brilliant and distinguished one. I have never heard a better Schubert [Symphony no. 9 in] C major, it was an excellent Rach[maninoff]-Pag[anini Variations] with Entremont I thought, balancing discretion and ardour; the [Bach] Brandenburg 3 I missed, but everybody is praising it as the most memorable in a long time, and the Marche Slav [by Tchaikovsky] made a terrific conclusion.

I am trying to unwind after all the excitement by writing a set of children's piano pieces before I resume work on a piece I began before for wind quintet and double-piano duet (i.e. two pianos eight hands).

All the twelve-tone boys liked the organ concerto, so it seems that I am really a *modern* composer against my will.

A better tribute than any piece of music is the reverence in which the orchestra holds you. Before I went on to play there were so many assurances from the men that whatever I did 'he' would follow, and that they would do anything for 'him'. To maintain discipline and to have that devotion is truly remarkable.

Please give Lady Boult my best wishes and thanks.

And again many thanks for everything.

> Yours,
> Malcolm

P.S. Chappell's renewed my contract for two years on the strength of the performance. MW

The stream of letters continued from composers whose works Boult conducted – many with detailed notes of performance. But an equally old interest was also attracting more attention – the teaching of conducting. One distinguished pupil who had been considering the art with the aid of Boult's handbooks was Yehudi Menuhin.

Highgate, London, N.6.
18th June, 1963.

Dear Adrian,

I have just read the two books on conducting which have clarified many points and the benefit of which I hope will be noticeable in my future efforts in this field! Both these books are written with such clarity and kindness and are so immensely to the point, that I wanted to tell you how grateful I am to you now more than ever before and to thank you too for the kind words you have to say about me.

I have noticed the increased accuracy and the importance of the stick with larger groups, as well as with precision music – as one might call works of Stravinsky. On the other hand, I have also noticed how much more expressive are the movements of the hands without the stick, which I still prefer for smaller classical works, especially as I do not use a stick and the bow is too long(!) when I play the violin concertos with my little Orchestra. Perhaps you would allow me to ask for a few hours of your time one of these days to help me with your great experience and immense technique.

I have tried a cork-handled stick, which I found much more comfortable and better balanced than one with a small knob at the bottom. I would particularly like to have one of yours. Could you tell me where I could get one?

Diana joins in much love to you and Ann,

> Always your very devoted
> Yehudi

Royal Station Hotel, York
22 June 1963

Dear Yehudi.

How lovely to get your letter & hear that the books had been useful. I should immensely enjoy talking with you about it all. That Porteous stick that I describe in the book has stopped – the only man who could make them has died. I am very angry with Chesters for letting it drop, & have written to say so, & now await their reply. I can't believe that no one else can make them. I shall also tackle Boosey & Hawkes if Chesters are no good.

Now will your secretary please ring Mrs Beckett, Langham 8202 (it is my office, 13 Queen Anne St, W.1.) & tell her when you have a spare moment, & I will greatly look forward to it.

We were sad to miss Bath [Festival] this year – full of silly dates, & couldn't fit it in.

Much love to you both from us both –
Yrs always
Adrian

A few months later came the death of Paul Hindemith. Boult's letter of sympathy brought a note from the composer's widow with a Christmas card which had now a touching interest.

Blonay sur Vevey
March 17th 64

Dear Sir Adrian,

Please forgive these belated words of gratitude. Your spontaneous messages of friendship and deep sympathy touched my heart.

I thought you might like to have the Christmas-card – his last opus – he designed it for the friends before he fell ill. You will find some last greeting for yourself. The Organ is an allusion to his new Organ-Concerto. If you wonder about the lion – it is my portrait for the initiated.

Thanks for the Clipping. You left out, that you own the
Manuscript [of the *Trauermusik*] and why!
   All best to you –
                   Gertrude Hindemith

1963
Fröhliche
Weihnacht
und ein
glückliches
Neujahr
1964

Paul und
Gertrud
Hindemith

1963
Merry
Christmas
and a
happy
New Year
1964

From Gustav Holst's daughter Imogen came a letter in response to Boult's query about tempi in the 'Dargason' movement of the *St. Paul's Suite*.

9 Church Walk, Aldeburgh, Suffolk.
Aug. 18 65

Dear Adrian,

I *certainly* agree that the Dargason should be the right speed for dancing! I have vivid memories of struggling to play it (2nd Horn) in S.P.G.S. orchestra[1] on Thursday afternoons with my father conducting, and then the following weekend dancing it on the Vicarage lawn at Thaxted, & 'thinking' some of the St Paul's Suite accompaniment while dancing, & finding to my joy that it fitted.

I think most string orchestras take it too fast. A few weeks ago I was doing it with the R.A.F. (as the Finale to Suite no 2 for Military Band) and I was afraid they'd want it quicker than the dance speed, but to my delight I found they *insisted* that it shouldn't be too quick!

I think the Dargason's ♩. is about 120. And I don't think it ought to accel, as the counterpoint with Greensleeves should feel the same both times: – also the end, with its dialogue between top & bottom, should be neat & precise.

120 is about the speed of the 2/4 crotchet in the quick bits of the *third* movement. But I think the Jig is quicker; – say ♩ = 132. And at [9] Piu mosso about ♩ = 148; – and then the accel for the last few bars one-in-a-bar ♩. = 84 increasing to 96

Much love to both,
Imogen.

After another series of rehearsals and performances with Yehudi Menuhin, Boult ventured a suggestion which Menuhin was to take up.

13, Queen Anne Street, London, W.1.
3 May 1966

Dear Yehudi,

When you read this you will say 'Adrian is even more

[1] Holst had written *ad lib* parts for the school orchestra.

182

cracked than usual', but I'm going on, & please just *don't answer* if you aren't interested.

I'm cracked enough to wonder – just to wonder, if I couldn't tell you one or two things about your *approach* to performance, both conducting *and* playing, that might help, although surely you have thought about all this again & again. Better men than I have illuminated my vision now & again, & I just wondered whether any of it might perhaps be of use. The serene perfection of your performance of the [Beethoven] Romances at the rehearsals was something that one *must* perpetuate if it can be done, & I'm sure it can.

If you think it at all worth while having a talk, do you ever pass by the BBC (we are across the road here)? Perhaps Miss Addison Smith could suggest something to Mrs Beckett? But you may well be too busy to be bothered with it, & I shall quite understand.

Hundreds of people have spoken to me about Tuesday. It *was* a wonderful privilege to take part with you in it.

With much love to you both
Yrs always
Adrian

A broadcast of the Brahms First Symphony with the Orchestra elicited the following from the distinguished horn player Barry Tuckwell.

121 Hamilton Terrace, London, N.W.8.
6th November, 1966.

Dear Sir Adrian,

It is with sadness that I confess to finding performances of music I know, boring and unsatisfying, I would prefer to look rather than to listen.

I must tell you what elation your performance of Brahms One has just given me. I tuned in at random and identified the orchestra but could not think who was conducting. I was completely gripped by the majesty of the interpretation, and the names I thought of just did not fit – during the last movement I *knew* it was you.

I am already embarrassed about writing this letter so I will go out and post it right away before I lose courage.

Thank you – I had begun to think it was *me*, maybe I am not so cynical and bored after all.

Yours sincerely
Barry Tuckwell

The old skill was there too for a cycle of the Beethoven Piano Concertos with the Russian pianist Emil Gilels, who wrote a rare letter of appreciation in English.

(25/9 Gorki Str., Moscow) London.
17/vii 67

Dear Sir Adrian,

It has been a great honor for me to play the five Beethoven concertos with you in London and I would like to express to you my grateful thanks for your imaginative and complete cooperation.

I hope it will not be too long before we have the opportunity of working together again.

With warmest greetings to you and Lady Boult.

yours
Emil Gilels

Later that summer the Boults had an invitation from his old B.B.C. chief Lord Reith who had recently been appointed Lord High Commissioner to the General Assembly of the Church of Scotland.

Lollards Tower   London SE 1
August 29 1967

Dear Sir Adrian,

Your letter of the 24th came today.

Yes, we were very sorry that you didn't accept the Holyrood invitation. There were many leaders of professions and industry and engineering, but no musicians.

The Lord High term of office is just for the fortnight in May. My being asked to give the inaugural address for the Festival wasn't connected with the L H C post. I was offered the Lord High appointment exactly 25 years ago, but declined it then. I am glad to have had this experience.

I hadn't seen or heard anything of the wretched play you wrote about – and wasn't it put on by the so-called Fringe organisation? The Festival authorities have no responsiblity for that, as you will know.

I am sure there's nothing you could say or feel about the intellectual & ethical depravity, which is put across nowadays, that I wouldn't agree with. I referred in St Giles to 'the vulgar ballyhoo of mass materialism and the irresponsibility and degradation of so much of the mass media communication.'

But I don't contemplate action on this general issue, or as it affects the Edinburgh Festival. And for this reason if no other – it would immediately involve me in comment on the principles, standards and general responsibility of the British Broadcasting Corporation. I've been under great pressure to say what I feel in that connection, but have so far stood off. It is probably better, and more 'decent' that I should, however much criticism it brings on me. (There is little obvious[*] today of the old quality of 'decency', is there?)

Yours sincerely,
J.C.W. Reith

* in life generally I mean.

In the New Year's Honours Boult was made a Companion of Honour. Among his congratulators was an old family friend, Lord Maclean, who had been made a Knight of the Thistle.

Duart Castle, Isle of Mull.
15th March 1969.

My dear Ann.

Oh dear! Oh dear! I am so very ashamed of myself that I have not written to you both before now to congratulate Adrian on his splendid C.H. – and now you write to me about my 'Thistle' – thank you so very much for your thought of us.

We were more delighted about the C.H. than we have been over any other friends who have been honoured by The Queen during past years.

No-one will ever know what millions of people have received comfort and joys – discovery – and heart searchings – and friendships from Adrian's unlimited determination to give his 'all' – all the time. I know he will wish to share his honour with you, just as I have given Elizabeth a 'great chunk' of my thistle!

Our love and deep admiration go to you both – I wish we could meet more often.

Yours ever,
Chips.

And from one of the oldest friends, Sir Thomas Armstrong, Principal of the Royal Academy of Music:

Newton Blossomville, Turvey, Bedford
April 6th 1969

My dear Adrian

It's hard to realize that more than fifty years have passed since I first began to hear of you from [Dean] T. B. Strong [at Christ Church, Oxford], who used to speak of the astonishment with which he had heard you say, in your interview as a freshman, that you intended to be an orchestra conductor. And this wonderful anniversary, with the honour and affection that surrounds you, is a testimony to the single-minded and concentrated idealism that has guided your great career.

Hester and I want to express to you something of our admiration and affection, and to tell you of our gratitude for all that you are and have done. We wish you many happy returns of the day, and much joy, in the present, and on your birthday, and for the future. We send our love to Ann and yourself, and wish you both to know how deeply we value the privilege of your friendship and the inspiration of your example.

Yours ever
Tom Armstrong.

On 9th April came Boult's 80th birthday. At the end of that year there was a concert at the Royal College of Music to commemorate the centenary of Hugh Allen's birth. At the end of the concert Boult directed a performance of the *Dona nobis pacem* from Bach's B minor

186

Mass. This was done as Allen had done it: disregarding the editor's markings, he began as softly as possible and made a steady crescendo through the work to finish fortissimo. Afterwards came this letter from Boult's friend and fellow-pupil of Allen's, Frank Howes:

Newbridge Mill, Standlake, Witney, Oxon.
Dec. 9/69

Dear Adrian

Dona nobis pacem was the experience of a lifetime, the product, I dare say, of a lifetime's experience. That marvellous opening started tears in my eyes in 4 bars & as the fugue proceeded the tears didn't stay in my eyes. I don't remember any comparable experience in my life, though I am not immune to tears sometimes in the Meistersinger quintet. I think many people in that hall were similarly moved.

Ys ever
Frank

Through these later years Boult's EMI gramophone recordings have been produced by Christopher Bishop, with Christopher Parker as balance engineer. 'We three are a team,' Boult says, 'and without them all these records would have been impossible for me.' After finishing the taping of Vaughan Williams's *Pilgrim's Progress*, Christopher Bishop wrote this letter:

4/5 Grosvenor Place, London, S.W.1.
25. Nov. 70.

Dear Sir Adrian,

You say I mustn't reply to your letter about *Pilgrim*, but I must disobey! It was very kind of you indeed to write, and it is of the greatest satisfaction to me to know that you approved of the casting and didn't find the chopping-up of the work [into recording sections to accommodate schedules of solo singers and chorus] too troublesome.

For my part I can only say how immensely I enjoyed the sessions quite the easiest and most musically satisfying opera sessions I've done. I've loved the *Pilgrim* since my Cambridge days, and there was a certain crusading joy about recording it, especially with John Noble.

187

I have played the first 2 acts through, and I can tell you that all has come out marvellously, and I know you will be pleased. It is splendid to hear the magnificent 1st Act as a 'sweep' – and that is all your doing – as is all the musical excellence, of course.

Thank you so much for all your patience during the morning about technical problems we had. How I wish we could now record some more operas! How about *Sir John in Love*?

We are looking forward to Sunday very much.

With best wishes to you both,

Ever,
Christopher.

A little over a year later the first copies of the *Pilgrim's Progress* recordings were out. One of the most enthusiastic responses came from Michael Kennedy, whose biographical works on Vaughan Williams and Elgar have achieved international recognition.

3 Moorwood Drive, Sale, Cheshire.
13.ii.72

Dear Adrian,

I have spent a thrilling weekend immersed in listening to the *Pilgrim* records, and must now send you this brief note not merely of congratulations but of very heartfelt thanks for so nobly, convincingly and incontrovertibly vindicating Ralph's belief in the power of this music of his. You really make it properly dramatic – in the music itself – and colourful; the pace is so well varied and I never felt there was too much of one mood, not even in the Evangelist scenes. The whole cast & orchestra supported you wonderfully, but it is all due to you really, and I only wish Ralph could know of this tremendous demonstration of your devotion to his art. Perhaps there is a musicians' paradise somewhere and 'hither the echoes come'.

Now, another great task awaits you – [Elgar's] *The Apostles*. Can't EMI be moved on that one?

Our love to you both – I am so deeply moved by these records & hope you fully realise what a superb thing you have done.

Michael.

EMI were moved at last to add *The Apostles* to the list of previously unrecorded English masterpieces available on records.

Meanwhile in November 1971 the London Symphony Orchestra had been conducted by the Prime Minister, Edward Heath, in a performance of Elgar's *Cockaigne* Overture. Boult sent congratulations, and received two letters – one from Edward Heath and another from his secretary Robert Armstrong (the son of Sir Thomas Armstrong).

10 Downing Street, Whitehall.
2 December 1971

Dear Sir Adrian,

Thank you for your letter of 29 November. I am grateful to you for your comments about the Festival Hall Concert. It was a great pleasure to have the opportunity to conduct such a superb orchestra.

I hope I remembered all the points in your own admirable book on conducting.

Yours sincerely,
Edward Heath

10 Downing Street, Whitehall.
9 December 1971

Dear Sir Adrian,

Thank you very much for your letter of 1 December, which the Prime Minister much enjoyed.

I have heard of people having two strings to their bow before, but never two bows to their stick. The Prime Minister did in fact have two sticks; the casualty rate at rehearsals was very high.

Yours ever
Robert Armstrong

In 1972 an old recording of Gustav Holst himself conducting *The Planets* was reissued. Boult wrote to the composer's daughter Imogen to ask her opinion of it.

9 Church Walk, Aldeburgh, Suffolk.
Feb 1 '73

Dear Adrian,
Do PLEASE forgive me for my long delay in replying to your letter.

And *thank you* for having written.

I think the chief 'revelation' in the tempi of G's recording of the Planets was the flow and continuity, *most* of the way through most of the movements, without any of the 'holding back to make a point' before big moments which some other conductors (NOT you!) have indulged in during the past 30 years, and which have made unwanted 'joins' in the music.

The speed of the opening of *Venus* was a reminder that his written 'Adagio' could often be an 'Adagio quasi Andante' in his own mind.

I find the speed of *Mars* as I can remember him doing it in the Queens Hall – *BUT* this is only MY memory of it! I remember watching him practice conducting this when I looked through the glass door of his sound-proof room at St Paul's, & I remember thinking 'If he does it any quicker, the crotchet will be too quick to *walk* to.' But here again, it is only *my* memory of it.

I think there is no doubt whatsoever that the extreme discomfort of the recording conditions and the agony of having to go *on* (because they weren't allowed to stop) must have distracted him on many occasions. My chief disappointments are *Mercury* and *Neptune*. I think *Uranus* is superb. And the legato continuity of the low-lying flutes in the slow march in *Saturn* is very impressive.

I think it would be quite wrong for anyone to think of this recording as 'authentic': he himself learnt a lot about conducting it as the years went by, and the way he did it for instance at the Cheltenham 'Holst' festival in the late 20s was already different in several ways from this recording. And I think if he had lived as long as Ralph [Vaughan Williams] lived, he would have made further changes in the way he conducted it. And I think it would be a great mistake for conductors to

190

imitate what he does in this 1926 recording. But I still find the record a revelation – as it gives such a clear impression of what the composer was doing with the work at that particular moment in history.

Once more, my *very* real regrets for having kept you waiting for a reply to your letter.

With love to you both, and every possible good wish, from
Imogen.

Frederick Ashton's ballet of Elgar's *'Enigma' Variations* brought Boult again into the theatre pit. One performance shared the bill with a work danced by Margot Fonteyn. He wrote to thank her for the beauty of her dancing, and received this letter:

In flight to New York
June 6th 1973

Dear Sir Adrian,

I am so deeply touched by your letter as I had wanted to speak to you too at the Coliseum but for some reason felt shy. It always seemed that either you or I were about to conduct or go on stage and it didn't seem the right moment.

I did stay in the wings a lot during *Enigma* and it was quite incredibly beautiful under your inspiration. Please forgive me for not coming to tell you so.

Very sincerely
Margot

Boult's 85th birthday in April 1974 was another anniversary marked by many letters. One came from a former student who recalled the conducting classes at the Royal College of Music half a century earlier – Michael Tippett.

Nocketts Hill Farm, Derry Hill, Calne, Wiltshire
Monday evening

My dear Adrian,

I did not realise it was yr 85th birthday till turning on the radio this evening – some recordings of yours. So, not a congratulatory telegram, but a letter. One of the pieces played was Brahms 3. You won't remember (tho I do, as it were yesterday) my standing beside you at the rostrum at the

RCM during a term's (?) training of that piece. (The cellos always had trouble with 2nd subject of the finale!) It's a long time ago. But what I learnt, as a composer, through those 4 years of Fridays at yr side, is nobody's business. A belated thank you – & for much beyond. But please don't reply.

Yr
Michael

For a broadcast concert nearly a quarter century after his retirement from the B.B.C. Symphony Orchestra, Boult chose the First Symphony of Sir William Walton. True to his custom, he once again consulted the composer on his work's performance.

La Mortadella, Forio d'Ischia.
Oct 12th 1975

My dear Adrian,
Though your letter is dated 28 Sept. it only reached here the day before yesterday, so my letter is somewhat belated.

I can't tell you how delighted I am that you are conducting my 'first' for the B.B.C. I've been thro' the work with your 'Nixa' record & tho' the record 'qua record' is abysmal, you've got it all right.

The answers to three questions are right & the metronome markings correct – perhaps the 'Maestoso' in the last movement might be a shade less so. The parts marked B.B.C. parts should be correct. I warned Christopher Morris (the new head of O[xford] U[niversity] P[ress] Music Dept.) that they should be checked so I think everything will be all right on that side & if the performance (which I am sure it will be) is even nearly as good as the record it should be a splendid performance & I am only too sorry that I am unable to be present.

I've been having an interesting & enjoyable time with [Elgar's] the 'Apostles' & the 'Kingdom' neither of which I had heard before. I like them both more than 'Gerontius' – perhaps your new recording [of *The dream of Gerontius*] will convert me! I hope so for I find Elgar's choral works rather inferior to the orchestral ones.

Apart from a chronic attack of sciatica which I am suffering

192

from at the moment I [am] keeping on the whole very well if not very musically productive. Very glad to hear of your recovery.

Yours ever
William

Several performances of the Elgar Violoncello Concerto were planned with the French 'cellist Paul Tortelier. One was played at York Minster on 19th June 1976 – with Tortelier attired in a canary yellow suit because the airline had misplaced the luggage containing his dress clothes. Another was to take place in the Waterloo Chamber of Windsor Castle on 28th September. A third programme, to include also one of Tortelier's own Concertos, was contemplated for Worcester Cathedral in the following summer. Tortelier's response was immediate.

Nice
27.7.76

Dear Sir Adrian,
So many thanks for your *lettre pétillante*!

Do I dream or do you mean really that I would have my own concerto played in Worcester Cathedral under your baton? Supposing my interpretation of your written words is right, I should have to ask two things at once: the first being 'Which concerto of mine?' because I have written *five* ones – 1 for piano and orchestra (my last work) one for violin and orchestra, two for cello and orchestra and one for 2 cellos and orchestra, – the second being: 'Would it be possible to postpone this concert as I shall be in the U.S.A. in July 1977?'

Concerning the second point, may I suggest a direct contact between the Worcester people (by this I mean the 'Accountants' of the organizing firm) and Emmie Tillett who knows better about my calendar from September 1977 onwards than I do myself!

If Air France, Lufthansa or BEA do not loose my luggage once more I ought to appear in a decent *frac* rather black than anything else next time we meet in Windsor. In order to make it sure, I have managed to left one of these *fracs* in the Tillett office, 124 Wigmore St., so, there should be no problem, whatever happens. (To be honest, I did not 'leave' it at Tillett's – I forgot it there!! Why? Because in my distrust of the luggage service in connection with airways company, I decided to carry my *frac* by hand . . . You see the result!)

Anyway, in Windsor I would rather wear two *fracs* rather than none.

With all best wishes and *mes hommages à* Lady Boult.

Yours sincerely
Paul Tortelier

That summer there was a 'Prom' performance of Elgar's First Symphony, which brought a letter from Robert Ponsonby, the B.B.C. Controller of Music.

B.B.C., Yalding House, 156 Great Portland Street, London, W.1.
29/vii [1976]

Dear Adrian,

it was a privilege and a joy to hear your Elgar last night. I could not be more grateful. You bring to that symphony a poignant strength which I've never heard with any other conductor. And the orchestra makes a quite individual sound for you. How much I – and many many others – look forward to your Wagner and Brahms, the Pastoral and (next season) the Great C major.

I was *delighted* to see you looking so well and *very* grateful to you for such a marvellous contribution to the Proms.

With all best wishes,

Yours ever
Robert

In February 1977 a Jubilee Concert at the Royal Albert Hall celebrated the 25th anniversay of The Queen's accession. The programme was shared by Richard Attenborough, Malcolm Williamson (conducting a setting of specially composed verses by the Poet Laureate Sir John Betjeman), and Boult, who conducted the *Orb and Sceptre* March which Walton had written for the Coronation in 1953. Malcolm Williamson, who succeeded Arthur Bliss as Master of the Queen's Musick, wrote after the concert:

17 Thornton Hill, London, S.W.19
11.ii.77

Dear Sir Adrian,
    . . . It was wonderful to see you in such dynamic form giving us the Walton with so much youthful ginger and effortless control. Dickie Attenborough & I were terrified and your kindness & advice put heart into us. Even so I find it extraordinary that the R.P.O. believe that a composer can automatically conduct. I cannot. Arthur said that he became so excited by his music that he accelerated. I slow down to enjoy my own scoring. But the R.P.O. is first class, & I am reminded of your saying once 'Any fool can conduct the Vienna Philharmonic!'[1] So any novice can conduct the R.P.O. They gave maximum goodwill, and my time went v. well. I wish poor old Betjeman had been there. He came out of hospital to a volley of press abuse. Please give my warm regards to Lady Boult. Yrs gratefully
                                        Malcolm

    Boult's 'Prom' performances in 1977 included Arthur Bliss's *Music for Strings*, the Elgar Second Symphony, and Malcolm Williamson's Organ Concerto. Bliss's widow wrote about *Music for Strings:*

8, The Lane, Marlborough Place, London, N.W.8.
Aug 3 1977

My very dear Adrian,
    How pleased Arthur would have been last night by your fine performance of *Music for Strings*! I shall never forget the happiness he expressed when he listened to your EMI recording of it barely three years ago; and last night would have made him just as delightedly content. I was in the hall *and* (thanks to modern magic) able to make a tape of it at the same time, so this morning I have had the pleasure of your performance all over again.

---

[1] In response to a query from Boult about an inexperienced conductor in Vienna, Egon Wellesz replied: 'Any fool can conduct the Vienna Philharmonic so long as he doesn't disturb them.'

195

My love to you and Ann – I go to France this morning but on my return I hope you both will let me see you
Trudy

About the Elgar performance there was a letter from Ernest Hall, the first trumpeter of the London Symphony Orchestra when Elgar himself conducted a recording of the Symphony in 1927.

114. Kings Hall Road, Beckenham, Kent
August 3rd/77.

Dear Sir Adrian.

I feel I must write to you to say how delighted I am, to read of your wonderful achievements during the last week or so, & also to congratulate you (if I may) on your health & stamina, to be able to conduct & concentrate as you are doing. May it continue for a long time yet!!

I heard your rendering of Elgar No 2 which brought back happy memories, when Sir Edward asked me at a recording why I held my top B♮ over to the next bar, & I replied that I was so pleased to get the note I didn't like to leave it. His reply was, – I intended to write it so, but thought it would be too high to hold.

Well I won't bore you any more only again to say how happy I am to see you still active. Am pleased to say Molly & I keep well, & have a lot to be thankful for.

Remember us kindly to Lady Boult & both send our very best wishes to you both.
Very sincerely
Ernest Hall

And after the Williamson Organ Concerto, the composer-soloist wrote:

510 Ben Jonson House   Barbican E.C.2.
9.viii.77

Dear Sir Adrian,

Well, what do you think of the stone that the builder forgot in 1961 becoming the head of the corner in 1977? We can thank Lady Boult for having faith in that little organ concerto. How critics change – even if not for the wiser. . . .

196

I am so grateful to you for keeping me in one piece. The clarity of the beat is superb; but beyond that you make us all feel like adults being given a framework, a discipline within [which] we can be expressive and flexible. Any shortcomings of mine were when I failed to look in the mirror and see the beat.

It gave us all pleasure to read the four excellent notices in the dailies. Trying to remember past occasions when a comparable wave of love was given by the public to an artist I can recall best Robert Mayer's birthday concert recently, and AS *best* all the past Boult appearances.

Please give my warmest good wishes to Lady Boult,

Your grateful
Malcolm

Boult's successor as director of the London Philharmonic Orchestra was Bernard Haitink. On Haitink's resignation after ten brilliant years with the Orchestra, Boult wrote to thank him for all he had done for music in London.

34 Cadogan Place, London, S.W.1.
23 November 1977

Dear Sir Adrian,

May I thank you very much for your kind words, specially from you that means a lot to me.

I am a great admirer of your work: please go on!

Yours truly
Bernard Haitink

He had gone on, and despite inevitable difficulties of illness and age he is going on still. As these lines are written he is planning to conduct Elgar's ballet *The Sanguine Fan* at the Coliseum in June 1978. But after the echoes of those performances have fallen silent, there will remain the inspiration of his example to enrich our civilisation. The last witness in this book is also the youngest. The 27-year-old conductor Jonathan Del Mar raised again in the spring of 1978 the central question of artistic execution – form *versus* detail. He had been studying Walton's First Symphony from the score which had assisted the performance of 1975.

5 Cumberland Street, S.W.1.
March 23 1978

Dear Sir Adrian,

I am ashamed of myself for having kept your score of the Walton Symphony for so long. . . . But I *have* now been through the Walton – and fascinating it was to see Sir William's own letters on the Symphony. Now when must I give you your score back – when would this be convenient to you?

A little problem about musical ethics which I should be fascinated to discuss with you. In Berlin, in September of last year, I heard the Pastoral (Beethoven's) under Karajan. The first movement was fast – but not intolerably so, the only pity being that he observed not a single repeat in the entire concert. But the second movement was terribly fast – impossibly fast – at about ♩ = 60, as I remember. Again in the Scherzo I felt with regret the lack of repeat, while the last movement (the Storm was excellent and/though! conventional) was again faster than I have ever heard or imagined it. Unbearable? I don't know. Maybe these are all details, because it was only afterwards, while we were applauding, – no, perhaps already by the last bars of the symphony – that I realised what Karajan *had* achieved: a glorious, an incomparably beautiful whole. We had for the first time experienced the whole symphony as one perfectly moulded arch, and the moving realisation of that experience forced me to condone his seeming lack of integrity over the details, however large the details seemed at the time or seem now.

Is it right to consider that maybe Beethoven did misjudge it and that the slow movement is too long ever to be integrated successfully into the piece as a whole, so that certain details may have to be sacrificed for the sake of a perfectly balanced whole?

I have experienced a similar feeling over the slow movement (considering it this time just by itself) of the Schubert Great C major [Symphony]. This time it was Haitink (at the Albert Hall) who shaped it into a whole and made me ask myself what all the fuss was about – it went beautifully, effortlessly, nothing laboured, and no one was looking at their watches. I went home convinced that this was the way, that it must always *flow*, and so on – until I heard Gerd Albrecht (on the radio) with the Zürich Tonhalle. Suddenly I realised that he was discovering a whole range, a new deeper level of emotions and expressions in the movement, all of which I knew Haitink had simply glossed over. Instead of just flowing beautifully, it was sustained beautifully, and the sheer intensity of expression, the *Innigkeit* that he produced in that movement, were something which it seems a crime consciously to sacrifice. Yet at the end of the movement one was too bound up with the intense drama played out in the last 20 bars to be able at all to appreciate a sense of having heard the movement as a whole. Haitink, it seems, chose the whole: Albrecht the parts. Are the two really mutually exclusive? *Can* one not achieve both? It would seem a terrible admission of defeat – and yet, have you ever heard both achieved together? In the Pastoral I fear it really is impossible – and so here comes the agonizing question – which? How can one possibly choose?

With very best wishes to Lady Boult and yourself from
Jonathan Del Mar.

Adrian Boult's answer had been found, perhaps, many years earlier in St. Paul's Epistle to the Philippians. When the B.B.C. asked him to identify a favourite quotation from the Bible, he broadcast it.

Finally, brethren, whatsoever things are true, whatsoever things are honest, whatsoever things are just, whatsoever things are pure, whatsoever things are lovely, whatsoever things are of good report; if there be any virtue, and if there be any praise, think on these things.

INDEX

201

204